STYLE AS STRUCTURE AND MEANING

William Bradford's Of Plymouth Plantation

Floyd Ogburn, Jr.

UNIVERSITY
PRESS OF
AMERICA

Copyright © 1981 by

University Press of America, Inc.

P.O. Box 19101, Washington, D.C. 20036

Library of Congress Catalog Card Number: 80-5879

83-640

TO

TREVIA AND KENYON

PREFACE

This study offers a very unconventional method of accounting for structure and meaning in a rather unconventional work--William Bradford's Of Plymouth Plantation. Indeed, few considerations are more problematic and crucial to the study of colonial American literature than structure and meaning. Far too often, colonial American poetry, captivity narratives, journals, sermons, and histories have been valued solely for their ideas or content; it is my hope that this study provides a method for appreciating their form as well.

Many people were instrumental in the completion of this work. I am especially grateful to Professor Robert D. Arner of the University of Cincinnati, who directed this study as a dissertation, offering invaluable scholarly advice. Similarly, Professors William Lasher and Dallas Wiebe, both of the University of Cincinnati, made many perceptive and helpful suggestions. I am also deeply indebted to Professor June Pauszek of the University of Cincinnati and the members of her Word Processing/Text Editing class (Ms. Clarinda Drake, Ms. Jenny Fellows, Ms. Lyn Dungan, Ms. Felicia Martin, Ms. Linda Saylor, and Ms. Anita Williams) for their adept typing of the manuscript; a special thanks to Ms. Linda Saylor, who worked especially hard on the manuscript. Finally, I thank Ms. Karen Cobb of the University of Cincinnati, who also helped type the manuscript.

Needless to say, I alone am responsible for whatever shortcomings this study may have.

Floyd Ogburn, Jr.
University College

ii

TABLE OF CONTENTS

Introduction

Few critics would agree that there are places in <u>Of Plymouth Plantation</u> where sentences "lack unity and are replete with dangling phrases and clauses" and are incoherent and lack direction.[1] Even fewer would agree that the "narrative is not highly structured."[2] Many critics feel that Bradford's history is an American classic, perhaps the first significant contribution to American literature--the most important work of seventeenth-century America, as Alan B. Howard has said.[3] Many also agree that the history has a discernible unified structure, although they differ as to what that structure is. Moses Coit Tyler, for example, says simply that the history is orderly, lucid, and instructive.[4] E. F. Bradford contends that the method of organization in general is annalistic and that events are arranged not merely on the basis of chronology but also on the basis of cause and effect.[5] Peter Gay admires the artistry but feels the history ends in elegy and silence.[6] John Griffith argues that the history's fundamental pattern is that of the American success story.[7] John J. Fritscher suggests that Bradford "arranges much of his material to dramatize the Calvinistic belief in direct intervention by injecting brief moral vignettes of a rise and fall pattern."[8] Alan Howard feels that the "reversal through recognition and submission, and the ascent which measures the force of God's sustaining hand, is the architectonic shape of the entire history."[9] David Levin believes that the organization is dialectical, cyclical, and alternating.[10] Jesper Rosenmeier argues that the structure grows out of Bradford's frequent perception of events as analagous to Christ's death and resurrection.[11] And Robert Daly contends that the Deuteronomic Formula is a pertinent aspect of structure but feels that the history's major structural pattern is the progression from a public to private document.[12]

What all critics recognize, either implicitly or explicitly, is that the nature of <u>Of Plymouth</u>

Plantation makes difficult any assessment of its structural unity. For the history contains problems with which it is not easy to work: Bradford obviously truncates his history, leaving blank the pages from 1647 and 1648, and there are changes in tone which seem to affect the book's unity. The great confidence that fills Book I and the annals from 1620 to 1632 is itself a unifying device, but the despair and, as Robert Daly has said, "elegiac tone" of the remaining annals detract from the book's coherence.[13] In short, _Of Plymouth Planta-tion_ is a very complex work, and its method of organization is not always very apparent.

Despite these kinds of structural problems, this study argues that Bradford's history is tightly unified and structured in a unique manner. By combining a number of traditional literary and stylistic methods with two stylistic tools, foregrounding and collocation, I hope to present a new approach to the history--an approach that should prove helpful in my attempt to account for a unified and coherent structure.

Geoffrey Leech defines foregrounding as "motivated deviation from linguistic, or other socially accepted norms."[14] In an article discussing the usefulness and implications of foregrounding as a tool for literary analysis, M. H. Short includes the following definition: "'the use of the devices of the language in such a way that this use itself attracts attention and is perceived as uncommon.'"[15] John Spencer and Michael J. Gregory say that collocation

> is set up to account for the tendency of certain items in a language to occur close to each other, a tendency not completely explained by grammar. For example, the item "economy" is likely to occur in the same linguistic environment as items such as "affairs," "policy," "plan," "program," "disaster." . . . These items are termed the collocates of "economy" which, because it is the item under examination, is itself termed the nodal item.[16]

2

For the most part, items become deviant or foregrounded for Leech and Short only as they depart from the norms of language in general. For me, however, an item becomes foregrounded as it deviates from the norms (that is, the major stylistic characteristics) of the context (Of Plymouth Plantation) within which it appears. Such a restricted definition gives me control and limitation: to talk about the norms of a history presents problems, but to talk about the norms of language presents an almost overwhelming task.

I have also elected not to use Leech's division of foregrounding into paradigmatic and syntagmatic because I am using foregrounding only to find the foregrounded or aberrant passage(s). I believe that the aberrant passage often represents the stylistic or rhetorical center of a work. This belief is crucial to this study. I contend that a rhetorical center is the chief way in which Of Plymouth Plantation achieves a unified and coherent structure--that the foregrounded or stylistic center establishes structural patterns and devices of unity and coherence from which all other paragraphs evolve. The idea that Bradford's history contains a stylistic center is implicit in much sound criticism of it. For instance, E. F. Bradford, Howard M. Jones, Peter Gay, Kenneth Murdock, David Levin, and Ursula Brumm go almost unconsciously to the landing passages at the end of Chapter 9 when analyzing the book's unity and structure.[17] Though many of them stop short of tying the stylistic devices in the landing passages to other passages, they offer many helpful insights.

Speaking of American literature in general, Richard Poirier makes a very perceptive observation, one which is directly related to the notion of a stylistic center:

Thinking of environment in American books as comparative units of space and time, a reader makes an obvious and very poignant discovery. What we remember about a book or a writer--and this is notably true in American literature--

is often the smallest, momentary revelations
that nonetheless carry an "enormous sense
of inner authority."[18]

In Bradford, it is the foregrounded passages
that carry the "enormous sense of inner authority"
which dominates all preceding and remaining parts,
giving them unity and structure; it is the foregrounded passages that function much like a thesis
sentence.

Also crucial to this study is the belief
that chronology has little or no relationship to
unity and structure in the history. While chronology and causal relations are present, Bradford
views events episodically as a series of tableaux,
each of which contains the whole truth, reveals a
unique aspect of God's plan, and represents a
unique point--a juncture at which the divine plan
can be seen from a new angle, as John F. Lynen has
argued convincingly.[19]   I approach, then, the
history mainly through episodes. The foregrounded
paragraphs--because they constitute the stylistic
center and establish patterns of meaning, unity,
and structure for all preceding and succeeding
parts--represent the major episode. I select six
additional episodes (two from the beginning,
middle, and end) and compare their stylistic
characteristics with those of the foregrounded
paragraphs.

Therefore, the study proceeds in the following manner: Chapter 1 provides an identification
of the foregrounded passages with an explanation of
why they are foregrounded, a brief contextualiza-
tion of the foregrounded paragraphs, a scansion of
the first one with the emphasis on stress groups,
and an intrasentence description of other significant stylistic features of the foregrounded paragraphs. Chapter 2 contains an intersentence
description of the stylistic features and a description of the unity, coherence, meaning, and
structure suggested by the foregrounded passages.
Chapter 3 applies collocation to the foregrounded
paragraphs to confirm the stylistic features

already noted and to get at additional principles of meaning and structure. Chapter 4, which discusses stylistic devices in roughly the same order as in the previous chapters, provides an analysis of other paragraphs, showing how their stylistic features evolve from those of the foregrounded paragraphs. This chapter is followed by a conclusion.

The general approach to prose style in this study is indebted to many critics.[20] The general format and various stylistic insights are based on Frank J. D'Angelo's fine analyses of the prose style of fiction and the essay.[21] I am also indebted to Edward Corbett's studies of classical rhetoric, especially his studies of Swift's prose style.[22] The idea that the basic relationships in sentences can be graphically depicted by cutting sentences in such a way as to reveal their structural affinities comes from D'Angelo and Francis Christensen.[23] However, my graphic representations differ from those of D'Angelo and Christensen, primarily because Bradford's sentences are not like the cumulative sentence they speak of. In fact, few of Bradford's sentences are cumulative. In using graphic representation, I have tried to place parallel and balanced elements directly beneath one another. For instance, I try especially hard to place the connectives and couplings beneath one another. Though I have not succeeded in all cases because of the complexity of sentence structure, what I have tried to do is to devise a method that will help in appreciating Bradford's parallel and balanced style.

Finally, I should say something about the words style and stylistics. There is little consensus among linguists as to what constitutes style (or stylistics for that matter). Richard Ohmann, for example, defines style "as part of what we ordinarily call meaning, that is peripheral meaning, or subterranean meaning, or connotative meaning,"[24] or "style is a way of writing."[25] Seymour Chatman contends that "a writer may be said to have style insofar as the choices he makes form a pattern which is relatively homogeneous and

recognizable."[26]   And Louis T. Milic suggests
that even the writer is on shaky ground when
he talks of his own style (e.g., as James does)
because he has little awareness of what mechanism
is involved in the stylistic decisions he is
constantly required to make. Style, then, becomes
mainly an unconscious process.[27]

   Whether style is unconscious or represents
epistemic choice, I assume that the sentence is the
primary unit of style, "that whatever complex
apprehension the critic develops of the whole work,
that understanding arrives mundanely, sentence by
sentence,"[28] and that stylistics is a way of
interpreting literature by drawing upon linguistic
theory and procedures to investigate the language
of literature.[29]

Notes to Introduction

[1] Albert H. Marckwardt, American English (New York: Oxford University Press, 1958), p. 19.

[2] John Griffith, "Of Plymouth Plantation as a Mercantile Epic,"Arizona Quarterly, 28, No. 3 (1972), 233.

[3] Alan B. Howard, "Art and History in Bradford's Of Plymouth Plantation," William and Mary Quarterly, 28 (1971), 238.

[4] A History of American Literature 1607-1676, I (New York: G. P. Putnam's Sons, 1879).

[5] "Conscious Art in Bradford's History of Plymouth Plantation," New England Quarterly, 1 (1928), 156.

[6] A Loss of Mastery: Puritan Historians in Colonial America (Berkeley: University of California Press, 1960), p. 52.

[7] "Of Plymouth Plantation as a Mercantile Epic," 233.

[8] "The Sensibility and Conscious Style of William Bradford," Bucknell Review, 17 (1969), 84.

[9] "Art and History in Bradford's Of Plymouth Plantation," 246.

[10] "William Bradford: The Value of Puritan Historiography," in Major Writers of Early American Literature, ed. Everett H. Emerson (Madison: University of Wisconsin Press, 1972), p. 25.

[11] "'With my owne eyes': William Bradford's Of Plymouth Plantation," in The American Puritan Imagination: Essays in Revaluation, ed. Sacvan Bercovitch (London: Cambridge University Press, 1974), p. 99.

[12] "William Bradford's Vision of History," American Literature, 44 (Jan. 1973), 569.

[13] Ibid., p. 557.

[14] "'This bread I break'--Language and Interpretation," A Review of English Literature, 6, No. 2 (1965), 68. See also Leech's "Linguistics and the Figures of Rhetoric," Essays on Style and Language, ed. Roger Fowler (London: Routledge and Kegan Paul, 1966), p. 139.

[15] "Some Thoughts on Foregrounding and Interpretation," Language and Style, 6 (Spring 1973), 97.

[16] "An Approach to the Study of Style," Linguistics and Style (London: Oxford University Press, 1964), p. 73. See also Leech's "Linguistics and the Figures of Rhetoric," p. 143 and his "'This bread I break'--Language and Interpretation," pp. 67-68; and J. R. Firth's "Modes of Meaning," Papers in Linguistics 1934-1951 (London: Oxford University Press, 1957), pp. 190-214.

[17] See Bradford's "Conscious Art in Bradford's History of Plymouth Plantation, 133-157; Jones' O Strange New World (New York: The Viking Press, 1952); Gay's A Loss of Mastery: Puritan Historians in Colonial America (Berkeley: University of California Press, 1966); Murdock's "Colonial Historians," in American Writers on American Literature, ed. John Macy (New York: Tudor Publishing Co.), pp. 3-12; Levin's "William Bradford: The Value of Puritan Historiography," in Major Writers of Early American Literature (Madison: University of Wisconsin Press, 1972), pp. 11-31; and Brumm's "Did the Pilgrims Fall upon Their Knees When They Arrived in the New World? Art and History in the Ninth Chapter, Book one, of Bradford's History Of Plymouth Plantation," Early American Literature, 12, No. 1 (1977), 25-35.

[18] A World Elsewhere: The Place of Style in American Literature (New York: Oxford University Press, 1966), p. 14.

[19] The Design of the Present: Essays on Time and Form in American Literature (New Haven: Yale University Press, 1969), p.p. 52-75.

[20] For example, see James R. Bennett's Prose Style: A Historical Approach through Studies (San Francisco: Chandler Publishing Co., 1971); William Cappel's "Repetition in the Language of Fiction," Style, 4, No. 3 (1970), 239-244; Ronald Carpenter's "Stylistic Redundancy and Function in Discourse," Language and Style, 3, No. 1 (1970), 62-68; Colen S. Cass' "Two Stylistic Analyses of the Narrative Prose in Cozzens' By Love Possessed," Style, 4, No. 3 (1970), 213-238; Seymour Chatman's "New Ways of Analyzing Narrative Structure," Language and Style, 2(1969), 1-36; Chatman's "Stylistics Quantitative and Qualitative," Style, 1, No. 1 (1967), 29-43; Donald Cunningham's, John Herrum's, and E. K. Lybbert's "Semantic Recurrence and Rhetorical Form," Language and Style, 4, No. 3 (1971), 195-207; Harold Delisle's "Style and Idea in Steinbeck's 'The Turtle,'" Style, 4 (1970), 145-154; Erik N. Enkvist's "On the Place of Style in Some Linguistic Theories," Literary Style: A Symposium, ed. S. Chatman (Oxford, 1971), pp. 47-65; Roger Fowler's Style and Structure in Literature (Ithaca: Cornell University Press, 1975); Michael Grady's "On Teaching Christensen Rhetoric," English Journal, 61 (1972), 859-877; L. G. Heller's "The Structural Relationship between Theme and Characterization," Language and Style, 4, No. 2 (1971), 123-130; Jack Kligerman's "A Stylistic Approach to Hawthorne's 'Roger Malvin's Burial,'" Language and Style, 4, No. 3 (1971), 188-194; John Lord's The Paragraph: Structure and Style (New York: Holt, Rhinehart and Winston, 1964); Albert Marckwardt's American English (New York: Oxford University Press, 1958); Frank McConnell's "Toward a Syntax of Fiction," College English, 36 (Oct. 1974), 147-160; Richard M. Ohmann's "Literature as Sentences," Essays in Stylistic Analysis, ed. Howard S. Babb (New York: Harcourt Brace Jovanovich, 1972), pp. 353-361; Ohmann's "Generative Grammars and the Concept of Literary Style," in Linguistics and Literary

Style, pp. 258-278; Ohmann's "Speech, Action, and Style," in Literary Symposium, ed. S. Chatman (New York, 1971), pp. 241-254; Ohmann's "Speech, Literature, and the Space Between," New England Literary History, 4 (1972), 47-64; Michael Orth's "The Prose Style of Henry David Thoreau," Language and Style, 7 (1974), 36-54; Donald J. Ross' "Conceptual Network Analysis," Semiotica, 10 (1974), 1-17; N. A. Sayce's "Literature and Language," Essays in Criticism, 7 (April 1957), 119-133; Robert Scholes' Structuralism in Literature (New Haven: Yale University Press, 1974), Robert L. Walker's "The Common Writer: A Case for Parallel Structure," College Composition and Communication, 21 (Dec. 1970), 373-379; Ian Watt's "The First Paragraph of The Ambassadors: An Explication," Essays in Stylistic Analysis, pp. 275-292; Glen Love's and Michael Payne's Contemporary Essays on Style (Glenview, Ill.: Scott, Foresman, 1969); Rulon Well's "Nominal and Verbal Style," The Problem of Style, ed. J. V. Cunningham (Greenwich: Fawcett, 1966), pp. 253-259; and Leonora Woodman's "A Linguistic Approach to Prose Style," English Journal, 62 (April 1973), 587-603.

21 See D'Angelo's "A Generative Rhetoric of the Essay," College Composition and Communication, 25 (Dec. 1974), 388-396; "Imitation and Style," College Composition and Communication, 24 (Oct. 1973), 283-290; and "Style as Structure," Style, 3, No. 2 (1974), 322-362.

22 See Corbett's Classical Rhetoric for the Modern Student (New York: Oxford University Press, 1971); and "A Method of Analyzing Prose Style with a Demonstration Analysis of Swift's 'A Modest Proposal,'" in Contemporary Essays on Style.

23 See Christensen's Notes Toward a New Rhetoric: Six Essays for Teachers (New York: Harper and Row, 1967).

24 "Prologomena to the Analysis of Prose Style," p. 3.

[25] "Generative Grammar and the Concept of Literary Style," p. 259.

[26] "Stylistics Quantitative and Qualitative," p. 31.

[27] "Rhetorical Choice and the Stylistic Option: The Conscious and Unconscious Poles," Literary Style, ed. S. Chatman (London: Oxford University Press, 1973), p. 83.

[28] Ohmann, "Literature as Sentences," p. 232. For a good discussion of this subject, see Richard McLain's "The Problem of 'Style': Another Case in Fuzzy Grammar," Language and Style, 10, No. 1 (1977), 52-65.

[29] Julie Carson, "Proper Stylistics," Style, 8 (1974), 302.

Chapter 1

The Foregrounded Passages and

the Intrasentence Description

The foregrounded paragraphs appear at the end
of chapter 9. Coming as they do after the history of Pilgrim sufferings in England, the voyage
to Holland and the difficulties encountered there,
the complex agreements and articles made between
the adventurers and planters in preparation for the
voyage to America, the grand and perilous crossing
of the Atlantic, and the safe arrival at Cape Cod,
these paragraphs present Bradford's utter amazement at the Pilgrims' whole predicament:

But here I cannot but stay and make a
pause, and stand half amazed at this poor
people's present condition; and so I think
will the reader too when he well considers
the same. Being thus passed the vast ocean,
and a sea of troubles before in their preparation (as may be remembered by that which went
before), they had now no friends to welcome
them nor inns or much less towns to repair to,
to seek for succour. It is recorded in Scripture as a mercy to the Apostle and his shipwrecked company, that the barbarians showed
them no small kindness in refreshing them,
but these savage barbarians, when they met
with them (as after will appear) were readier
to fill their sides full of arrows than
otherwise. And for the season it was winter,
and they that know the winters of that country know them to be sharp and violent, and
subject to cruel and fierce storms, dangerous
to travel to known places, much more to search
an unknown coast. Besides, what could they
see but a hideous and desolate wilderness,
full of wild beasts and wild men--and what
multitudes there might be of them they knew
not. Neither could they, as it were, go up
to the top of Pisgah to view from this wil-

derness a more goodly country to feed their hopes; for which way soever they turned their eyes (save upward to the heavens) they could have little solace or content in respect of any outward objects. For summer being done, all things stand upon them with a weather-beaten face, and the whole country, full of woods and thickets, represented a wild and savage hue. If they looked behind them, there was the mighty ocean which they had passed and was now as a main bar and gulf to separate them from all the civil parts of the world. If it be said they had a ship to succour them, it is true; but what heard they daily from the master and company? But that with speed they should look out a place (with their shallop) where they would be, at some near distance; for the season was such as he would not stir from thence till a safe harbor was discovered by them, where they would be, and he might go without danger; and that victuals consumed apace but he must and would keep sufficient for themselves and their return. Yea, it was muttered by some that if they got not a place in time, they would turn them and their goods ashore and leave them. Let it also be considered what weak hopes of supply and succour they left behind them, that might bear up their minds in this sad condition and trials they were under; and they could not but be very small. It is true, indeed, the affections and love of their brethren at Leyden was cordial and entire towards them, but they had little power to help them or themselves; and how the case stood between them and the merchants at their coming away hath already been declared.

What could now sustain them but the Spirit of God and His grace? May not and ought not the children of these fathers rightly say: "Our fathers were Englishmen which came over this great ocean, and were ready to perish in this wilderness; but they cried unto the Lord, and He heard their voice

13

and looked on their adversity," etc. "Let
them therefore praise the Lord, because He
is good: and His mercies endure forever."
"Yea, let them which have been redeemed of
the Lord, shew [sic] how He hath delivered
them from the hand of the oppressor. When
they wandered in the desert wilderness out
of the way, and found no city to dwell in,
both hungry and thirsty, their soul was over-
whelmed in them. Let them confess before the
Lord His lovingkindness and His wonderful
works before the sons of men."[1]

These paragraphs combine description with reflection in a manner that is unmatched by any other
passage in the history. They are climactic,
carrying "an enormous sense of inner authority."
As Ursula Brumm has said, the landing passages
represent "the very apex of the whole book," with
"a section of description and reflection lodged
between sea voyage and land exploration."[2] If
the reader can remember only one thing from the
history, then certainly it will be the landing
passages.

The first stylistic feature that contributes
to the book's unity, coherence, and structure is
the rhythm created by the interplay of stress
groups. Only the first paragraph will be scanned,
since it is sufficient in length to make clear the
stress patterns.[3] Foot-divisions are based, for
the most part, on syntax and punctuation. In some
cases, accents and foot-divisions may be somewhat
tenuous, but, as Baum has said, scansion is not
wholly a key to the reading of prose; it is

only a basis of rhythm, not the rhythm, itself. Just as the metrical pattern of verse
does not represent the actual reading, but
the theoretic norm to which the language of
verse is adjusted, so these submetrical
patterns of prose rhythm represent--only at
what one might call two removes--an underlying
scheme, usually unconscious on the part of the
writer in the sense that they were not aimed

14

at, yet existent in the sense that they reveal themselves to the attentive ear.[4]

Therefore, it seems to me that there are some foot-divisions or junctures which are almost imperceptible but are present nonetheless because of the tendency of Bradford's prose to beat itself out in binary stress groups (the strong stresses that the many couplings receive are mainly responsible for this). There is also a tendency to run back-to-back, lengthy cadences which themselves are often controlled by the binary stresses of the couplings that they contain, even though many of the cadences consist of more than two stresses. Such foot-divisions are designated by a broken bar($\prime$).

In some cases, syllables or words have been marked as weak or secondary because they seem to distribute their stress to a syllable or word later in the sentence (this seems especially true of the cadences), thus contributing to the rising sensation so frequently felt in Bradford's prose.

As a final word of caution, the reader should remember that scansion is never a rigid process. Five different people scanning the same passage will inevitably get some conflicting results. Yet for each person who scans the passage, the results will be an accurate representation of the rhythm of that passage. Though the reader may scan some lines differently than I have, I do not feel that this will impair significantly the importance of the results obtained.[5]

Sentence 1 divides into stress groups of 1, 2, 2, 2, 3, 1, 2, 1, 1, and 2:

But here / I cannot but stay / and make a pause, / and stand half amazed / at this poor people's present condition;/ and so / I think will the reader,/ too,/ when he / well considers the same.

The couplings "but stay and make a pause, and
stand" are of a very complex nature. They do
not indicate clearly, as they will later in the
passage, the true relationship of the couplings
to binary stress groups. Yet one can see that
binary stress groups predominate, with three-stress
and one-stress groups helping to avoid monotony.
The stress groups are very balanced, breaking the
sentence into three major sections, each beginning
with an iambic foot. From the one-stress "but
here" at the beginning, the sentence rises to
several binary stress groups and continues this
upward movement into the alliterative three-stress
cadence at the middle of the sentence. The second
section falls again at the beginning (and so),
rises with a two-stress group, and falls to a
one-stress end. The last part of the sentence
starts with a one-stress group (when he) and concludes with a two-stress one.

Sentence 2 falls into stress groups of 4,2,2,
2,3,2,3,2,3,1,2, and 2:

Being thus passed the vast ocean, / and a sea of
troubles / before in their preparation / (as may be
remembered / by that which went before), / they
had now / no friends to welcome them / nor inns to
entertain / or refresh their weatherbeaten bodies;/
no houses / or much less towns to repair to, /
to seek for succour.

With sentence 2, the prose begins to expand and the
presence of the four-stress group in the first
division amplifies the image of the "vast ocean."
The sentence falls and levels for three consecutive
binary stresses, climbs again to a three-stress
group, returns to a binary stress, and concludes

16

(that is, the first major portion of the sentence)
with a three-stress group. As in sentence 1,
sentence 2 pivots on an iambic foot. Thus, the
second major division begins with the one stressed
"no houses," rises and concludes with two consecutive binary stress groups. One should also note
the distributed stresses in "in their preparation"
and "or much less towns" and how they contribute to
the rising movement.

    Pivoting on iambs, sentence 3 divides into
stress groups of 3, 2, 2, 2, 3, 3, 2, 2, 2, and
3:

It is recorded in Scripture / as a mercy to

the Apostle / and his shipwrecked company, /

that the barbarians showed them / no small

kindness in refreshing them, / but these

savage barbarians, / when they met with them /

(as after will appear) / were readier to fill

their sides / full of arrows than otherwise.

The balance of the stress groups is simply superb,
to say the least: a three-stress group is followed
by three binary stresses; two three-stress groups
fill up the middle. Exactly three binary stresses
follow and the sentence concludes with one three-
stress group, ending as it began. It should be
clear by now that the rhythm is basically of a rise
and fall or alternating nature and that the iamb
and anapest tend to occur more than any other type
of foot. Again, distributed stresses contribute to
the rising movement: "that the barbarians," and to
some extent "to fill their sides / full."

    The pattern of the stress groups in sentence
4 is 1, 2, 4, 3, 4, 3, and 4:

And for the season / it was winter, / and they
that know the winters of that country / know
them to be sharp and violent, / and subject to
cruel and fierce storms, / dangerous to travel
to known places, / much more to search an
unknown coast.

Present for the second time are stress groups of
four. This is due primarily to the fact that
rather lengthy rhythmic sequences (cadences) are
run back-to-back, creating an impression of ascen-
sion and expansion and acting out the difficulties
of searching "an unknown coast." Though the
cadences contain more than two stresses, their
rhythm still seems governed by the binary stresses
on the couplings within them: "sharp and violent,"
and "cruel and fierce." All stress groups are
balanced: the sentence rises from one and two-
stress groups to four and alternates from three to
four until the end.

1, 2, 3, 2, 3, and 1 is the pattern of the
stress groups in sentence 5:

Besides, / what could they see / but a hideous
and desolate wilderness, / full of wild beasts
and wild men-- / and what multitudes there
might be of them / they knew not.

The couplings "hideous and desolate" and "wild
beasts and wild men" continue to dominate the
rhythm. Even though a coupling may appear in a
foot-division that has more than two stresses, as
it does in the second foot-division, it somehow
seems to sound an even stronger stress. What
should be noted again is the balance of the

stresses--the rise and fall movements they suggest.
Indeed, the style is almost architectural, as if
Bradford is attempting to construct sentences as
one would a building.

The stress groups of sentence 6 are 2, 1, 3,
2, 4, 4, 2, 4, and 3:

Neither could they, / as it were, / go up to

the top of Pisgah / to view from this wilder-

ness / a more goodly country to feed their

hopes; / for which way soever they turned

their eyes / (save upward to the heavens) /

they could have little solace or content / in

respect of any outward objects.

The lengthy four-stress cadences pile up in the
middle and end, as they did in sentence 4, often
forming a climax or arch in the middle, since this
is where most of the three- and four-stress cadences occur. The juxtaposing of various stress
groups is closely allied with the Pilgrims' vertical and horizontal movements in time and space to
discern and comprehend complex realities. And the
four-stress groups often signify the most extreme
attempts at comprehension. For unlike Moses, the
Pilgrims cannot go up to the top of Pisgah to grasp
the complexities of the wilderness. As elsewhere,
the coupling in the four-stress cadence "they could
have little solace or content" carries the strong-
est of the four stresses.

3, 2, 2, 2, 3, and 4 is the pattern of the
stress groups in sentence 7:

For summer being done, / all things stand upon

them / with a weatherbeaten face, / and the

whole country, / full of woods and thickets,

represented a wild and savage hue.

The sentence alternates between two- and three-
stress groups and ends in three- and four-stress
cadences. The couplings in these cadences create
their usual effect.

Sentence 8 falls into stress patterns of 2,
2, 2, 3, and 5:

If they looked behind them, / there was the

mighty ocean / which they had passed / and was

now as a main bar and gulf / to separate them

from all the civil parts of the world.

Through gradation, the sentence rises from three
consecutive binary stress groups to one three-
stress and concludes with a four-stress one, as if
Bradford is attempting to capture the sound of
separation and isolation. The distributed stresses
in the second, fourth, and fifth foot-divisions
complement this rising process.

Sentence 9 divides into stress groups of 2,
3, 1, 2, and 2:

If it be said / they had a ship to succour

them, / it is true; / but what heard they

daily / from the master and company.

The sentence ends in a two-stress coupling; therefore, it ends as it began, as far as stress is
concerned. The sentence has rhythmic balance. The
one stress on "it is true" quietly de-emphasizes
this almost parenthetical, but confident assertion.

2, 2, 1, 2, 2, 2, 3, 4, 2, 4, 3, and 5 is the
pattern of the stresses in sentence 10:

20

But that with speed / they should look out a
place / (with their shallop) / where they
would be, / at some near distance; / for
the season was such , / as he would not stir
from thence / till a safe harbor was discovered by them, / where they would be, / and
he might go without danger; / and that victuals consumed apace / but he must and would
keep sufficient for themselves and their
return.

Rising and falling, the sentence rises in stately
fashion to the long five-stress cadence at the
end . Yet beneath these five stresses, the reader
hears the binary stresses on the coupling "must
and would" which are so basic to the rhythm of
this passage. The distributed stresses in the
second and perhaps fourth foot-divisions contribute to the rising movement.

Sentence 11 divides into stress groups of 2,
4, and 5:

Yea, / it was muttered by some ' that if they
got not a place in time, / they would turn
them and their goods ashore and leave them.

Again gradation is present: the sentence rises
from a two- to a four-stress group and concludes
with a five-stress one. This movement is enhanced
by the distributed stress in the third foot-division. The somewhat lengthy coupling in the last
foot-division subtly reminds the reader of the
basic rhythm of the passage, even though the foot-
division consists of five stresses.

The stress groups of sentence 12 are 3, 5, 3,
5, and 3:

Let it also be considered ; what weak hopes of

supply and succour they left behind them, /

that might bear up their minds ; in this sad

conditions and trials they were under; / and

they could not but be very small.

By now, to comment on the balance of stress groups
is to risk understatement. Especially clear here
is the very dominant role played by the couplings.
Note, for example, how the coupling in the long
second foot-division prevents one from breaking the
foot after the first word (supply) of the coupling.
But as a result of the rhythm generated by the
coupling, one is forced to leave it intact, even
when the result is a rather long foot.

1, 1, 4, 4, 5, 8, and 2 is the pattern of
stress groups for the last sentence of the paragraph:

It is true, / indeed, / the affections and

love of their brethren at Leyden ; was cordial

and entire towards them, / but they had little

power to help them or themselves; / and how

the case stood between them and the merchants

at their coming away ; hath already been

declared.

Like sentence 1, sentence 13 begins with a one-
stress group and ends with a two-stress one.
Occurring at various places in the sentence, three
couplings provide a final reminder of the basic

22

rhythm of the paragraph. The sentence rises by gradation from a one- to an eight-stress group and falls gently to a two-stress conclusion.

A consideration of other stylistic features of individual sentences reveals other devices of rhythm and emphasis and brings one closer to the meaning and the structural unity of the passages. Beginning with an adversative connective (but), sentence 1 moves through two additive connectives (and).[6] It is also a parallel and balanced sentence:

But here I cannot but stay
                and make a pause,
                and stand half amazed at this poor
                        people's present condition;
And so I think will the reader, too, when he well
    considers the same.

In fact, this sentence is more balanced and parallel than at first meets the eye. It has been shown above how "and so" is balanced against "but here" and how it (and so) is the pivotal point of the sentence. Although there is a slight inversion ("I think will the reader, too," and "when he well considers") in the "and so" clause, the clause is mainly a parallel restatement of the "but here" clause. For Bradford is assuming that the reader too "cannot but stay and make a pause, and stand half amazed at this poor people's present condition" when he considers the situation as Bradford has done. The balance and parallelism promote rhythm and emphasis.

Various kinds of repetitions also promote rhythm, emphasis, unity, and coherence. There is the repetition of individual words: "and" is repeated three times (polysyndeton), moving the items it joins into separateness and making them increasingly clear.[7] Since these items ("stay," "make a pause," and "stand") are synonymous or nearly synonymous (couplings), rhythm and emphasis are once again enhanced.

Sound patterns are also significant in sentence 1; they play a large role in making the sentence coherent. The alliterative /s/ sound in "stay," "stand," "so," and "same"; and the /p/ in "pause," and "poor people's present" bring attention to these words and establish a sense of continuity and tightness. Assonance in "stay," "make," "amazed," and "same" and the initial /k/ sound in "cannot," "condition," and "considers" do essentially the same thing.

Sentence 2 is almost perfectly parallel and balanced as it progresses from additive to alliterative connectives.[8] The alternative connectives ("nor," "or"), among other things, underline the idea of choice, possibility, and alternatives:

Being thus passed the vast ocean,
          and a sea of troubles
     before in their preparation (as may be
          remembered by that which went before),
     they had now no friends to welcome them
                    nor inns
                         to entertain
                    or refresh their
                         weatherbeaten bodies;
               no houses
                    or much less towns
                    to repair to,
                    to seek for succour.

The repetition of similar grammatical structures and individual words is fairly obvious. What seems significant in this sentence is the manner in which the repetition of similar grammatical structures and individual words contributes to sound and rhythm, perhaps the most important stylistic features of this sentence: the fricatives--the /v/ sound in "vast," the /š/ in "ocean," the /s/ in "sea," the /š/ in "preparation"--clearly establish the sound of the "vast ocean" and the metaphoric "sea of troubles." Then the alternative, anaphoric connectives (no, nor, or) near the end of the sentence add the image of the rising and falling waves.

24

Other alliterative patterns of note are "sea," "seek," and "succour"; and "went," "welcome," and "weatherbeaten." Distributed at almost equal distances in the sentence, they add unity, coherence, rhythm, and emphasis.

Moving from an additive to an adversative connective, sentence 3 is basically antithetic in structure. Implicit in this sentence is the concept of alternatives and possibilities: the experience of Paul versus the experience of the planters:

It is recorded in Scripture as a mercy to the Apostle

and [to] his shipwrecked company,
that the barbarians showed them no small kindness in refreshing them,
but these savage barbarians, when they met them (as after will appear) were readier to fill their sides full of arrows than otherwise.

Four prepositional phrases occur back-to-back early in the sentence: "in Scripture as a mercy to the Apostle and his shipwrecked company." "Barbarians" is the only word that is repeated.

As far as sound is concerned, the alliterative /s/ still tends to dominate: "Scripture," "small," "savage," and "sides." The sentence ends with an alliteration of the /f/ sound: "to fill their sides full of arrows than otherwise." Though not alliterative in all cases, there is also a prevalence of /k/ sounds, as in "recorded," "shipwrecked," "company," and "kindness." As with alliteration, the use of litotes ("no small kindness") results in emphasis.

Joined by all additive connectives, sentence 4 makes use of semantic alternation in its latter part (the two infinitive phrases):

```
And for the season it was winter,
and they that know the winters of that country
                know them
                        to be sharp
                            and violent,
and
                [to be] subject to cruel
                        and fierce storms,
        dangerous
                to travel to known places,
        much more
                to search an unknown coast.
```

Again repetition occurs at various levels. Similar
syntactic patterns (infinitives) are repeated: "to
be sharp and violent," to be "subject to cruel and
fierce storms," "to travel to known places," and
"to search an unknown coast," but an antithetic
relationship is established between the last two.
The repetition of "know" gives the sentence unity,
coherence, and rhythm. The use of the double
subject in "and for the season it was winter" adds
emphasis. The couplings "sharp and violent" and
"cruel and fierce" serve identical purposes,
although they restate words in terms of synonyms or
near synonyms. Polysyndeton and anaphora are
present in the repetition of "and."

On the level of sound, alliteration is quite
prevalent: "season," "subject," and "search"; and
"country," "cruel," and "coast." As in the above
sentences, these words are distributed at various
places in the sentence, giving it a tight and
rhythmic structure.

Beginning with an alternative connective
("besides") and turning on one additive connective,
sentence 5 consists of two parallel and balanced
clauses; choice (or the lack of it) is an inextri-
cable element:

```
Besides,
        what could they see but a hideous
                    and desolate wil-
                        d e r n e s s ,
```

full of wild beast
and wild men--
and what multitudes there might be of them
they knew not.

The pairing of the what clauses creates the same
kind of balance, rhythm, and emphasis as the
pairing in the couplings: "hideous and desolate"
and "wild beast and wild men." Note too that the
couplings are matched in the number of syllables.

Structured around two connectives, sentence 6
begins with the alternative connective "neither,"
which picks up on the element of choice present in
sentence 5:

Neither could they, as it were, go up to the top of
Pisgah
to view from this wilderness a
more goodly country
for which way soever they turned their eyes (save
upward
to the heavens)
they could have little solace
or content in
respect of any outward
objects.

Repetition does not play as significant a role as
it does in previous sentences. The only syntactic
structure that is repeated is the infinitive
phrase: "to view from this wilderness a more
goodly country" and "to feed their hopes." Few
individual words of note are repeated, with the
exception of the modal "could," which gives the
parts of the sentence an almost parallel structure.
There is also a kind of repetition (through the
use of the synonym) in the coupling "solace or
content."

Repetition of similar initial sounds is
quite prominent: the /k/ sound in "could," "country," and "content"; the /ð/ in "they," "the,"
"their," "this." Assonance is present in "go,"
"more," "hopes," "soever," and "solace."

27

Sentence 7 is organized around a causal ("for") and an additive ("and") connective:

For summer being done, all things stand upon them
    with a weatherbeaten face,
And the whole country, full of woods
                        and thickets,
        represented a
                            wild
                    and savage hue.

Perhaps the most important stylistic feature in this sentence is the use of "things" as the subject of the first independent clause. For the most part, subject slots up to this point have been filled by the narrator, "I," or the Pilgrims, "they." Now the Pilgrims become acted upon; "things stand upon them." Like the cadences which expand when the Pilgrims find it difficult to see and to comprehend "outward objects," the placing of the Pilgrims in the object slot emphasizes further the difficulty of their present predicament.

Though there is no repetition of grammatical patterns, there is significant repetition of individual words: "and" is used three times in the latter part of the sentence. The use of polysyndeton here creates emphasis and maintains the rhythm that has been clearly established by now. This sentence also contains two couplings: "woods and thickets" and "wild and savage." As E. F. Bradford has said, the couplings are neither redundant nor explanatory; they are used primarily for stylistic reasons--for emphasis and rhythm.[9]

On the level of sound, alliteration provides unity and coherence. The repetition of the /w/ sound in "with," "weatherbeaten," "woods," and "wild" ties this sentence together, much like the repetition of the w's in the march to Heorot passage in Beowulf. There is also the repetition of the /f/ sound in "for," and "full." Assonance is present in "done" and "upon."

Sentence 8 achieves balance mainly through the use of the if-then syllogistic structure. Once

28

again, the notion of alternatives and possibilities
is implied--to look behind them or not to look behind them:

If they looked behind them,
        there was the mighty ocean which they had passed
            and was now as a main bar
                            and gulf to separate them from
                                all the civil parts of the
                                                    world.

This sentence demonstrates well how the couplings
and the repetition of sound patterns provide unity,
coherence, and emphasis. The coupling in this
sentence occurs in the form of a simile: "as a
main bar and gulf." One other synonym is added in
the infinitive "to separate." Obviously this kind
of near repetition foregrounds this part of the
sentence, emphasizing the key idea of obstruction.

      Alliterative patterns reinforce the idea of
obstruction: "passed" and "parts"; "separate" and
"civil." Assonance also helps: "bar" and "parts."
Thus, the interplay of various stylistic devices
to isolate key concepts seems to be a major
characteristic of Bradford's prose.

      Sentence 9 is also structured syllogistically:

      If it be said they had a ship to succour them,
          it is true;
              but what heard they daily from the master
                                      and company?

The major sound pattern in this sentence is assonance: "if," "it," "ship," and "is." The latter
part of the sentence receives emphasis mainly
because it is placed in question form. As such, it
anticipates sentence 10. While "master and company" is not a coupling, it too receives emphasis
because it has the appearance of a coupling.

      Sentence 10 is a long series of main clauses
held together by adversative, causal, and additive
connectives. From this sentence until the end of

29

the paragraph, the reader is constantly made aware of the concept of alternatives, possibility, and choice:

But that with speed they should look out a place
    (with their shallop) where they would be, at
        some near distance;
For the season was such as he would not stir from
    thence till a safe harbor was discovered by
    them, where they would be,
and he might go without danger;
and that victuals consumed apace
but he must
    and would keep sufficient for themselves
                            and their return.

Giving order and balance to a seemingly unwieldy sentence, a "but" clause begins and ends the sentence. The repetition of "but" and "and" at the beginning of clauses is anaphoric. Although not an example of word repetition, the word "discovered" quickly directs the reader's attention back to "look out," helping to unify the first part of the sentence. There is the coupling "must and would"; it should be clear by now that a major function of the couplings is to promote emphasis and rhythm. Whether joining couplings, clauses, phrases, or other individual words, the almost obsessive use of "and" as a connective (polysyndeton) also promotes emphasis.

Sound devices also unify and highlight key concepts. There is assonance: "place," "safe," and "apace"; there are alliterative patterns with the /s/ pattern clearly predominating: "speed," "some," "season," "such," "stir," "safe," and "sufficient."

Sentence 11 achieves balance mainly through its resemblance to the if-then syllogism:

    Yea, it was muttered by some that
        if they got not a place in time,
        they would turn them
                and   their goods ashore
        and leave them.

30

Of particular note is the use of the passive voice.
As a result, the Pilgrims once again temporarily
become <u>receivers</u> instead of <u>doers</u>, objects instead
of subjects. Of special note also is the coupling
near the end of the sentence: "<u>turn</u> them and their
goods ashore and <u>leave</u> them" (emphasis mine).

Sentence 12 uses one additive connective to
join its two major divisions:

```
Let it also be considered what weak hopes of supply
                                    and succour
              they left behind them,
that might bear up their minds in this sad condition
                                    and trials
              they were under;
and they could not but be very small.
```

Notice how one's attention is forced to hover
momentarily over the first coupling: "supply and
succour." First, the coupling seems announced by
two preceeding words which have similar initial
sounds: "what weak." Then the coupling not only
forms an alliterative pattern itself, but it also
consists of two words which have an identical
number of syllables. The reader's attention pauses
next at the second coupling: "sad condition and
trials"; one can see how certain ideas receive more
attention than others in Bradford's prose.

Sentence 13 is a series of main clauses held
together by an adversative and additive connective:

```
It is true, indeed, the affections
              and love of their brethren at Leyden
              was cordial
              and entire towards them,
but they had little power to help them
              or              themselves;
and how the case stood between    them
              and              the merchants at
    their coming away hath already been declared.
```

The number of connectives in this sentence and in
Bradford's prose in general--whether they join main

31

clauses, phrases, or the items in the couplings--is simply amazing, especially the number of times "and" is used as a connective. Here, "and" occurs no less than five times.

A pertinent feature to observe from the outset of the second paragraph is the virtual disappearance of the element of choice, of alternatives. The imperative sentences (3, 4, and 6) take control. There is one choice, one alternative: "the Spirit of God and His grace." Thus, sentence 1 begins in question form (perhaps for rhetorical purposes only because the reader knows that there is only one possible answer):

What could now sustain them but the Spirit of God
                      and   His grace?

In light of what has preceded in the first passage (and the history in general),this question sounds almost facetious. Indeed, the people of Plymouth have no other logical alternative, that is, from the Pilgrims' point of view. Perhaps the most significant stylistic feature of this sentence is that the Pilgrims have been relegated to the object slot again. But instead of "all things" standing "upon them with a weatherbeaten face," this time they are acted or stood upon by God. For the declarative version of sentence 1 reads somewhat like the following: The Spirit of God and His grace could now sustain them.

On the level of sound, alliterative patterns focus attention on key words: note, for instance, how alliteration compels one to equate "sustain" with "Spirit" and "God" with "grace."

Sentence 2 has an antithetic structure and is unique in that it consists in part of an imaginary speech which is a fairly close paraphrase of Deuteronomy 26.5.7:

May not
and ought not the children of these fathers right-
      ly say: "Our fathers were Englishmen which
      came over this great ocean,

and were ready to perish in this wilderness;
but they cried unto the Lord,
and He heard their voice
and looked on their adversity," etc.

If one compares the original with Bradford's
paraphrase, he will soon discover one of the most
significant sources of Bradford's style.   For
instance, verse 5 of The Geneva Bible reads: "And
thou shalt answer & say before the Lord thy God, a
Syrian was my father, who being ready to perish for
hungre, went downe into Egypt, and soiourned there
with a smale companie, and grewe there unto a
nation great, mighty, & ful of people."   And verse
7:    "But when we cryed unto the Lord God of our
fathers, the Lord heard our voyce, and loked on our
aduersitie, and on our labour, and on our oppres-
sion."   What is common to both versions is the use
of polysyndeton and anaphora.   Both styles reflect
an almost obsessive propensity for connectives,
especially "and." And what is common to the biblical style and Bradford's in general is the extensive use of alliteration, assonance, repetition of
various syntactic patterns, repetition of key
words, and couplings.

The rest of the paragraph continues the
imaginary speech, this time paraphrasing selected
verses from Psalm 107.   Sentence 3 is tightly
structured in climactic order:

"Let them therefore praise the Lord,
because He is good:
and His mercies endure forever."

Other devices of coherence and unity are alliterative patterns: "them therefore" and "He" and
"His."

Sentence 4, like sentence 3, is imperative:

"Yea, let them which have been redeemed of the Lord,
shew how He hath delivered them
                                    from the hand
                                    of the oppressor."

The most pertinent stylistic feature is alliteration, which almost underlines some of the important words: "have," "how He hath," and "hand."

Sentence 5 makes use of the periodic structure:

"When they wandered in the desert wilderness
                out of the way,
        and found no city to dwell in,
            both hungry and thirsty,
    their soul was overwhelmed
                in them."

Semantic recurrence (as well as the periodic
structure itself) is the most prominent device of
unity, coherence, and emphasis.[10] To be sure,
"desert," "wilderness," "out of the way," "no city
to dwell in," and "hungry and thirsty" share part
of their collocational range. This, in turn, is
complemented by alliterative patterns: "wandered,"
"wilderness," "way," and "was": and "desert" and
"dwell."

    The last sentence returns to the imperative
mood and is almost perfectly parallel and balanced:

"Let them confess before the Lord His lovingkindness and His wonderful works
                before the sons of men."

On the level of the repetition of syntactic patterns, there are the "before" phrases; on the level
of individual words, there is the implied repetition (ellipsis) of "confess." A type of redundant
compound which recalls the couplings, "lovingkindness" obviously serves emphatic purposes. On the
level of sound, there is alliteration: "wonderful
works."

    Truly, Of Plymouth Plantation represents an
"art that conceals art."[11] It possesses a subtle
style. Because of the book's restrained diction
and ordered simplicity, the reader is frequently
lulled into believing that he is reading nothing

more than a simple and "plain" style. But Bradford's style is plain only in the sense that
schemes and tropes are not used for ornamentation;
complexly interwoven, however, they serve mainly to
promote rhythm, unity, coherence, meaning, and
structure by always bringing attention to and
isolating key stylistic features and concepts.

Notes to Chapter 1

[1]William Bradford, Of Plymouth Plantation, ed. Samuel E. Morison (New York: The Modern Library, 1952), pp. 61-63. Other references to this work will appear in parentheses after each quotation.

[2]"Did the Pilgrims Fall upon Their Knees When They Arrived in the New World? Art and History in the Ninth Chapter, Book One, of Bradford's History of Plymouth Plantation, p. 29.

[3]The following symbols will be used to denote the degrees of stress: (1) "⁄" for strong stress, (2) "`" for secondary and distributed stresses, and (3) "ᴗ" for weak stress. Works that have been particularly helpful in my study of stress in prose are: George Saintsbury's A History of English Prose Rhythm, 3d ed. (1912; rpt. Bloomington: Indiana University Press, 1967); Norton R. Tempest's The Rhythm of English Prose (Cambridge: Cambridge University Press, 1930); André Classe's The Rhythm of English Prose (Oxford: Basil Blackwell, 1939); Paull F. Baum's . . . the other harmony of prose . . . (Durham, N.C.: Duke University Press, 1952); Ian A. Gordon's The Movement of English Prose (London: Longmans, 1966); Marjorie Boulton's The Anatomy of Prose (London: Routledge and Kegan Paul, 1954); Regina M. Hoover's "Prose Rhythm: A Theory of Proportional Distribution," College Composition and Communication, 24 (Dec. 1973), 366-374; and James R. Bennett's Prose Style: A Historical Approach through Studies (San Francisco: Chandler Publishing Co., 1971).

[4]Baum, p. 91.

[5]Tempest, p. 24.

[6]See Louis T. Milic's "Connectives in Swift's Prose Style," Linguistics and Literary Style, pp. 243-255.

[7]See Winston Weathers' "The Rhetoric of the Series," Contemporary Essays on Style, p. 26.

[8]Milic, pp. 243-255.

[9]"Conscious Art in Bradford's History of Plymouth Plantation," New England Quarterly, 1 (1928), 142.

[10]See Cummings', Herum's, and Lybbert's "Semantic Recurrence and Rhetorical Form," Language and Style, 4, No. 3, (1971), 195-207.

[11]Kenneth B. Murdock, "Colonial Historians," in American Writers on American Literature, ed. John Macy (New York: Tudor Publishing Co., 1931), p. 8.

Chapter 2

The Intersentence Description

of Stylistic Relationships

At the intrasentence level, the following
stylistic tendencies were observed: (1) the use of
binary stress groups to establish a very distinctive and balanced rhythm, (2) the almost obsessive
use of connectives (polysyndeton) and the concept
of alternatives, choice, and possibility that is
shaped and underscored by them, especially the
alternative ones, (3) the use of couplings, (4) the
use of word or phrase repetition and synonyms, (5)
the use of analogy (typology), (6) the use of sound
patterns: alliteration and assonance, and (7) the
use of balanced and parallel structures. Though
not readily apparent at the intrasentence level,
there are two additional pertinent features that
surface at the intersentence level, and therefore,
must be included in the intersentence analysis:
(8) the movement from the visible to the invisible
and back to the visible world (this is partly
related to the use of metaphor) and (9) the shifting of the Pilgrims back and forth from subjects to
objects in surface structure. In this chapter, I
will trace each of these stylistic features in the
order they appear above throughout both paragraphs.

I

The following scheme will help the reader
recall the discussion of stress groups and appre-
ciate the interplay of the stress groups at the
intersentence level:

    (1) 1, 2, 2, 2, 3, 1, 2, 1, 1, 2
    (2) 4, 2, 2, 2, 3, 2, 3, 2, 3, 1, 2, 2
    (3) 3, 2, 2, 2, 3, 3, 2, 2, 2, 3
    (4) 1, 2, 4, 3, 4, 3, 4
    (5) 1, 2, 3, 2, 3, 1
    (6) 2, 1, 3, 2, 4, 4, 2, 4, 3
    (7) 3, 2, 2, 2, 3, 4

```
(8)  2, 2, 2, 3, 5
(9)  2, 3, 1, 2, 2
(10) 2, 2, 1, 2, 2, 2, 3, 4, 2, 4, 3, 5
(11) 2, 4, 5
(12) 3, 5, 3, 5, 3
(13) 1, 1, 4, 4, 5, 8, 2
```

Many critics have argued, and quite rightly, that Bradford's is a balanced style.[1] This balanced style orginates at the level of stress. As we examined the stress groups at the sentence level, we noted that they occurred systematically: binary stress group ruled, and they were manipulated so as not to create monotony; the stress groups rose and fell or alternated; this rise-fall movement was closely related to the Pilgrims' various degrees of vertical and horizontal movements in time and space to discern and comprehend complex realities, with the 4, 5 and larger stress groups frequently signifying the most extreme attempts at comprehension.

At the level of the paragraph, the manipulation of stress groups mirrors that at the level of the sentence. The whole concept of balance and system becomes clearer at the paragraph level: sentence 3 begins and ends with a three-stress group, sentence 5 begins and concludes with a one-stress group, sentence 9 with a binary stress group, and sentence 12 with a three-stress one. Some stress groups proceed wholly by gradation as in sentences 8 and 11. In others, roughly half of the sentences start by gradation and end in a variation or alternation of stress groups: sentences 1, 4, 5, 12, and 13.[2]

Both sentences 1 and 13 begin and end with a one and two-stess group, making the paragraph tight and neat. And the final binary stress group in sentence 13, coming as it does after the extraordinarily long eight-stress group, is the epitome of the rise-fall movement spoken of earlier in this study. Significantly, it occurs immediately before the first sentence of paragraph 2:

"What could now sustain them but the Spirit of God and His grace?" Indeed, to fall is what a Pilgrim should do before his God.

Thus, at the level of the paragraph, one could argue that the rhythm, as it grows out of the stress groups, rises and falls or alternates toward God, the sole concern of the second passage; and that this rhythmic movement is evident not only in the interplay of stress groups in individual sentences, but also in the contrast between the number of stress groups in each sentence.

II

Like the stress groups, the connectives are rhythmic devices, but they grow into a larger function. A scheme that lists intrasentence and intersentence connectives in both passages will prove helpful at this point:

(1) But . . . and . . ., and so . . .; and. . . .
(2) Being . . ., and . . ., nor . . . or . . .;
. . . or. . . . (3) . . . and . . ., but. . . .
(4) And for . . ., and . . . and . . ., and . . .
and. . . . (5) Besides, . . . but . . . and . . .,
. . . and . . . --and. . . . (6) Neither . . .;
for . . . or. . . . (7) For . . . and . . . and
. . . and. . . . (8) If . . . and . . . and. . . .
(9) If . . .; but . . . and . . .? (10) But . . .;
for . . . and . . .; and . . . but . . . and . . .
and . . . . (11) Yea, . . . and . . . and. . . . . . .
(12) . . . and . . . and . . .; and. . . but. . . .
(13) . . . indeed, . . . and . . . and . . . but
. . . or. . . and . . . and. . . .

(1) . . . but . . . and. . . . (2) . . . and. . .:
. . . and . . .; but . . ., and. . . . (3) . . .
because. . .: and. . . . (4) Yea, ... (5) When
. . . and . . ., and. . . . (6) . . . and. . . .

This scheme makes clear that intrasentence and intersentence connectives are used abundantly. In light of this, three questions come to mind: Why does Bradford employ connectives so extensively?

Was he conscious that he used them so elaborately?
What rhetorical purposes do the connectives serve?
The first two questions are somewhat difficult to
answer, but certainly they need to be raised.
Perhaps the answer to the first question lies in
the area of literary influences. Then certainly
the Bible, as has been shown above, plays a large
role. Since the early English colonists transported
with them the literary trends of that time,[2]
there is good reason to believe that Bradford was
also influenced by the Senecan-based prose style of
mid-sevententh century England. As the frequent
references to Cato, Seneca, and Pliny in Of Plymouth Plantation indicate, Bradford, like other
seventeenth century writers, had read the classics.
In the basic prose style of the middle years of the
seventeenth century, argues Ian Gordon,

> subordination is at a minimum. The sentence
> proceeds in what is virtually a series of main
> statements, each developing from the last.
> These are linked together in one of three
> ways: parataxis combined with juncture;
> coordination introduced usually by such words
> as "and," "but," "nor," "neither" or "for";
> and a kind of quasi-subordination, where the
> link-word is usually "as," "that," "where," or
> "which."[3]

Gordon could just as easily have said this of
Bradford.

For all practical purposes, Bradford is a
conscious artist. If nothing else, the couplings
act as a testament to this. He might not have
consciously inserted every connective that is
revealed in the scheme above, but he almost certainly was aware of his use of most of them. After
all, his preface does indicate that he is very much
interested in style.

Such an extensively connected prose, as
Louis T. Milic has argued about Swift's use of
connectives, creates an appearance of great logic.
Because the "reader does not realize that his
understanding is due to the redundant nature of the

connective guides, he reaches the conclusion that
the writer is eminently logical, transpicuously
clear, and economical with words to the point of
terseness." However, Milic continues, "it is
persuasiveness, not clarity, which results from
Swift's connectives. The enchainment of sentences
by means of connectives carries the reader along
with great mobility and induces him to believe in
the clarity and simplicity of what he has read."[4]

While Milic chooses persuasiveness over
clarity, I contend that they both are of equal
significance, at least as far as Bradford's connectives are concerned. For the two paragraphs quoted
above (and the history as a whole) constitute an
argument--an argument that is written in a "plain
style" (persuasively and clearly)--an argument that
is shaped and underlined by the connectives, especially the alternative ones. A cursory glance
at the scheme of connectives will verify the latter
point.

Sentence 1 of the first paragraph is an introductory sentence, and it also states the propo-
sition of the argument: the reader, like Bradford,
will "stand half amazed at this poor people's present condition" if he (the reader) "well considers
the same," that is, if the reader weighs the
difficulties that are about to be enumerated as
Bradford has weighed them. Sentence 1 begins with
the adversative connective ("but") and includes one
additive and one additive pleonasm ("and so").

Sentence 2 states the first difficulty that
the Pilgrims encounter, and the notion of alternatives, possibility, and choice is accentuated by
the alternative connectives in the latter part of
the sentence: "they had now no friends to welcome
them nor inns to entertain or refresh their
weather-beaten bodies; no houses or much less towns
to repair to, to seek for succour" (emphasis mine).

This in itself is enough to "stand half
amazed at," but in order to persuade the reader to
accept his point of view, Bradford specifies even

42

further in sentence 3. Sentence 3 picks up on the
concept of possibility in sentence 2, but this time
it is clearly possibility denied:

> It is recorded in Scripture as a mercy to the
> Apostle and his shipwrecked company, that the
> barbarians showed them no small kindness in
> refreshing them, but these savage barbarians,
> when they met with them (as after will appear)
> were readier to fill their sides full of
> arrows than otherwise. (emphasis mine)

The Indians could have greeted the Pilgrims ami-
ably, as the barbarians greeted Paul. But of
course the Indians do not.

Sentence 4 is comprised of all additive connectives. This sentence is suggestive of the way
this paragraph (and many of the paragraphs throughout the history) works. It proceeds deductively by
accretion: the first sentence is a generalization;
the second sentence gives a specific example of the
first. There is little genuine subordination.
Main clauses are added with each clause further
concretizing the preceding one, and all clauses
point back to the first one. But the overriding
relationship between these main clauses, as we
shall see, is one of choice, possibility, and
alternatives.

Sentence 5 begins with an alternative connective ("besides"), which is followed by one adversative ("but") and two additive connectives ("and"):
"Besides, what could they see but a hideous and
desolate wilderness, full of wild beasts and wild
men--and what multitudes there might be of them
they knew not." Clearly the paragraph is pro-
gressing from one choice or possibility to another.
But all too often, what results is the rather odd
choice of one, which itself is frequently undesir-
able: as the Pilgrims look out over the wilderness, the only thing that they can perceive is "but
a hideous and desolate wilderness."

As far as paragraph progression or movement is concerned, sentence 6 is extremely significant. It is the rhetorical center of the paragraph; it maintains the notion of choice and possibility, indicating the only real alternative that the Pilgrims have and thus simultaneously providing an early insight into paragraph movement or structure; it underscores the Pilgrims' complex predicament:

> Neither could they, as it were, go up to the top of Pisgah to view from this wilderness a more goodly country to feed their hopes; for which way soever they turned their eyes (save upward to the heavens) they could have little solace or content in respect of any outward objects.

Momentarily, the parallel between the type (Moses) and the antitype (Pilgrims) is broken. The break in the parallel emphasizes the primacy of spiritual vision (the eye of faith) as opposed to mere literal sight. Historically (that is, typologically) considered, Moses glimpses the Promised Land only from afar because his faith in God's promise is finally not strong enough. The outcome for the Pilgrims will be quite different, for even in this "hideous and desolate wilderness" (the historical reality) they can detect the sustaining presence of God. Unlike Moses, then, they cannot climb to the top of a mountain to grasp the complex realities of the American wilderness. The only real alternative is to look toward "the heavens." And this is where the paragraph is going. It alternates from one earthly alternative or choice to another, finally arriving at the one sustaining heavenly choice--God. And of course, there is nothing odd about God being a choice of one.

Beginning with a causal connective, sentence 7 adds concrete details to sentence 6. It makes clear, as the remainder of the sentences in this paragraph also do, that the Pilgrims have no other alternative but God. Even nature seems against them: "all things stand upon them with a weather-beaten face, and the whole country, full of woods and thickets, represented a wild and savage hue."

Sentences 8 and 9 both use "if" as a major connective. Both sustain the notion of alternatives and continue concretization of the Pilgrims' predicament. In sentence 8, there is the image of isolation: "the mighty ocean" acts "as a main bar and gulf to separate them from all civil parts of the world." In sentence 9, they cannot even rely absolutely on their ship for aid, and the beginning adversative connective ("but") in sentence 10 initiates the reason: the captain will not land until he finds a safe harbor, and he can only share a limited amount of the ship's food with the Pilgrims, keeping the rest for the return voyage.

Beginning with the quasi-connective "yea," sentence 11 depicts a steadily worsening situation. The Pilgrims are running out of alternatives: "if they [the captain and crew] got not a place in time, they would turn them and their goods ashore and leave them."

Sentences 12 and 13 are comprised of additive and adversative connectives. The sentences undercut the Pilgrims' last earthly alternative. They cannot turn to their "brethren at Leyden" because they (the Leyden people) "had little power to help them or themselves."

Sentence 1 of the second paragraph reveals the Pilgrims' only alternative, the direction toward which the extensively connected prose of the first paragraph has been progressing--faith in things unseen, in God: "What could now sustain them but the Spirit of God and His grace?" Wrapped in biblical analogy, the rest of this paragraph is a sustained paean to God as the ultimate alternative.

Hence, meaning and structure (especially as they are shaped by the connectives) work together to formulate a persuasive and clear argument, which is essentially this:

And well might it make them remember what the Psalmist saith, Psalm cxviii.8, "It is better

45

to trust in the Lord than to have confidence
in man." And Psalm cxlvi, "Put not your trust
in princes," (much less in merchants) "nor in
the son of man, for there is no help in them."
(p. 101)

This is a note that resounds throughout the history.

III

As the first passage moves towards the sec-
ond--creating a structure whose most characteristic
feature is the alternation from one choice or
possibility to another, finally arriving at God as
the only genuine possibility--the couplings, because
of their abundance, help make the argument more
persuasive and grow into a reinforcing structural principle:

1. stay and make a pause, and stand
2. vast ocean, and a sea of troubles
   no friends . . . nor inns
   to entertain or refresh
   no houses or much less towns
   to repair to, to seek for
4. sharp and violent
   cruel and fierce storms
5. hideous and desolate wilderness
6. solace or content
7. full of woods and thickets
   wild and savage hue
8. main bar and gulf to separate
10. must and would keep
11. turn them and their goods ashore and
    leave them
12. hopes of supply and succour
    sad condition and trials
13. affections and love
    cordial and entire
1. Spirit of God and His grace
2. May not and ought not
6. His lovingkindness and his wonderful works

From this list of the couplings in both paragraphs, three things should be emphasized, some of

which are obvious but pertinent nonetheless. First, each coupling is constructed in the nature of a series. Most of the series are of a two-part nature; that is, most connectives link two items. Winston Weathers has done an interesting study of the series. He argues that:

> the series--as a result of the number of items it contains, the presence or absence of conjunctions within it, and the degree of parallelism in its presentation--functions rhetorically in a number of different but simultaneous ways. By manipulating the series in three different areas at once, the writer can determine what sort of intellectual or emotional appeal he wishes to make to his audience.

Therefore, Weathers continues, a writer can construct the

> two-part series and create the aura of certainty, confidence, didacticism, and dogmatism. He can write the three-part series and create the effect of the normal, the reasonable, the believable, and the logical. He can write the four-or-more part series and suggest the human, emotional, diffuse, and inexplicable.[5]

The various effects that Weathers speaks of are probably not consciously sought after by Bradford, but it seems to me that it is this kind of critical thinking that explains in part the stylistic effect of the couplings. The first sentence of paragraph 1 contains a three-part series: "stay and make a pause, and stand," creating the effect of the normal, the credible. The second sentence consists of five two-part series; it is a catalog of two-part series. Instead of functioning like the individual two-part series, sentence 2 functions more like the four-or-more part series; that is, the general effect of sentence 2 is of "the human, emotional, diffuse, and inexplicable." Such a view seems in accord

with the tone of the first two sentences. The
first sentence is an introductory one that almost
casually asks the reader to ponder with the narrator. But the second sentence shifts to the
emotional, and to a certain extent, the inexplicable and illogical. After the Pilgrims have
crossed the "vast ocean, and a sea of troubles,"
they find it particularly frustrating that there
are neither friends, inns, entertainment, refreshment, houses, nor towns to greet them upon landing.
Of course one could argue here that Bradford is
being terribly naive and that he should not have
expected anything else. But from the Pilgrim point
of view, this predicament is easily explained and
yet not so easily explained; it is one that is
easily comprehended and yet not so easily comprehended. As a member of God's chosen people, the
Pilgrims had already suffered tremendous hardships
in England, Holland, and on the voyage to America.
In short, even from the point of view of a chosen
people who should expect a certain amount of
suffering (testing), the additional difficulties
that greeted them at landing would be ones to
"stand half amazed at."

Although there is an air of certainty that
stems from the prevalence of two-part series
throughout the remainder of this paragraph, it is a
certainty of the futility of looking for alternatives and possibilities among men. Bradford is
certain that it is vain to put one's trust in
man--that God is the only real alternative to
whatever plight man finds himself in. Recall the
early parenthetical acknowledgement of this in
sentence 6: (save upward to the heavens). And of
course the final acknowledgement comes in the
two-part series of sentence 1, paragraph 2:
"Spirit of God and his grace."

This consideration of the couplings as items
in a series leads to the second thing that should
be emphasized: the relationship between the couplings (as items in a series) and structure. I
suggest that the structure that emerges from both
paragraphs is a movement from the normal and

48

logical (sentence 1, paragraph 1) to the almost
abnormal, the inexplicable, and the illogical (the
rest of paragraph 1 which relates the difficulties
of finding alternatives), and back to the normal
(all of paragraph 2, which pictures God as the only
alternative). If nothing else, the systematic
repetition of the couplings in almost every sentence transforms them into a structural principle.

The final thing to be emphasized in looking
at the list of couplings is their similarity or
near similarity of meaning. It might not be too
farfetched to argue that the synonymous nature of
the couplings is tied directly to the notion of
alternatives. The very nature of many of the
couplings seems to deny choice. Though many of
them consist of two or more items, there is only
the appearance of two's and three's. There is, for
instance, little difference between the items in
"stay and make a pause, and stand," "sharp and
violent," "cruel and fierce," "hideous and desolate," "wild beasts and wild men," "solace or
content," "wild and savage," "main bar and gulf to
separate," "supply and succour," "affection and
love," "cordial and entire," "Spirit of God and His
grace," and "His lovingkindness and His wonderful
works." A first item may be more inclusive in
meaning than a second one (or vice versa), but the
first one usually contains the second as a part of
its meaning. Consequently, the reader faces the
same denial of choice in some aspects of the
language of the paragraph as the Pilgrims faced
upon landing.

IV

Other words and phrases are repeated (or
synonyms are used) almost as systematically as the
couplings. But while the couplings function mainly
as structural devices, word repetition operates
primarily as a device of coherence, unity, and
meaning.[6] The following list of words or phrases
that are repeated in both paragraphs indicates how
pertinent repetition is to paragraph unity and
coherence:

1. stand

2. passed, vast ocean, refresh, weatherbeaten bodies, to repair, to seek,
   succour

3. barbarians, showed, refreshing, savage
   barbarians, appear, full

4. season, winter, winters, to travel, to
   search

5. see, wilderness, full, wild men

6. go up, to view, wilderness, goodly country, feed, hopes, turned, eyes, upward
   to the heavens, outward objects

7. summer, stand, weatherbeaten face, country, full, savage

8. looked, passed, mighty ocean

9. succour, it is true, heard

10 look out a place, season, discovered,
   danger, victuals

11 place, turn

12. hopes

13. It is true, to help, stood

1. sustain, God

2. fathers, great ocean, wilderness, Lord,
   heard, looked on

3. Lord, good

4. Lord, shew, deliver

5. wandered, desert wilderness, found, to dwell, hungry and thirsty

6. Lord

The word "stand" is repeated three times: sentences 1, 7, and 13, paragraph 1; "passed" twice: sentences 2 and 8; "ocean" with various modifiers three times: sentences 2 and 8 of paragraph 1, and sentence 2 of paragraph 2; "weatherbeaten" twice: sentences 2 and 7, paragraph 1; "succour" twice: sentences 9 and 13, paragraph 1; "barbarians" twice: sentence 3, paragraph 1; "savage" twice: sentences 3 and 7, paragraph 1; "full" three times: sentences 3, 5, 7, paragraph 1; "season" three times: sentences 4, 10, and 12, paragraph 1; "wilderness" four times: sentences 5 and 6, paragraph 1, and sentences 2 and 5, paragraph 2; "country" twice: sentences 6 and 7, paragraph 1; "looked" three times: sentences 8 and 10, paragraph 1, and sentence 2, paragraph 2; "Lord" or "God" six times: sentence 6, paragraph 1, and sentences 1, 2, 3, 4, and 6, paragraph 2; and so on.

Synonyms are used extensively also and some words are even synonyms of the words mentioned above. The infinitive phrases "to repair" and "to seek" in sentence 2, paragraph 1 have synonyms in sentence 4, paragraph 1 ("to travel" and "to search"); in sentence 6, paragraph 1 ("go up"); in sentence 10, paragraph 1 ("look out" and "discovered"); and in sentence 5, paragraph 2 ("wandered"). "See" in sentence 5, paragraph 1, has synonyms (collocates is probably more appropriate) in sentence 6, paragraph 1 ("to view," "eyes . . . upward to the heavens," and "outward objects"); in sentence 2, paragraph 1 ("to seek"); in sentence 10, paragraph 1 ("look out"); in sentence 4, paragraph 2 ("shew"). "Feed" in sentence 6, paragraph 1, has synonyms or collocates in sentence 10, paragraph 1 ("victuals") and in sentence 5, paragraph 2 ("hungry and thirsty").

Repetition simply glues these paragraphs together, making them function as one. Practically

51

all words and phrases in paragraph 1 are repeated
either directly or in the form of a synonym; the
same is true of paragraph 2. All of the words in
paragraph 1 lead directly to paragraph 2: the lack
of nourishment, friends, inns, good weather, a safe
harbor, and a trustworthy "master" in paragraph 1
is more than made up for in the sustaining power of
"the Spirit of God and His grace" in paragraph
2. And finally, such an extensive use of repetition is tied directly to meaning. Almost without exception, it is the key words that are repeated over and over again, as we shall see in the
discussion of collocation in chapter 3.

V

Like the binary stress groups, the connectives, the couplings, and word repetition, the
analogy introduced in the first passage progresses
toward the second, reaching its culmination there.
John F. Lynen has observed that for the Puritan

> the most natural form of thought is analogy,
> and it is therefore not surprising that anal-
> ogy is the dominant characteristic of Puritan
> literature. No other trait is so important,
> no other literary method so all pervasive,
> for analogy is not merely a stylistic device
> but the very method and design of Puritan
> thought--a mode not only of interpretation
> but of having the experience to be inter-
> preted.[7]

This is true not only of the two passages presently
under investigation, but also of Bradford's entire
history.
The first use of analogy occurs in the reference to Paul in sentence 3, paragraph 1:

> It is recorded in Scripture as a mercy to
> the Apostle and his shipwrecked company, that
> the barbarians showed them no small kindness
> in refreshing them, but these savage barbar-
> ians, when they met with them (as after will
> appear) were readier to fill their sides full
> of arrows than otherwise.

Because all biblical characters and events are significant to Bradford, this reference to Paul is important, but not as important as the reference to Moses in sentence 6, the pivotal sentence in this paragraph:

> Neither could they, as it were, go up to the top of Pisgah to view from this wilderness a more goodly country to feed their hopes; for which way soever they turned their eyes (save upward to the heavens) they could have little solace or content in respect of any outward objects.

This sentence features the sort of typology that is characteristic of the history. There is a close parallel between the epic journey of the people of Israel and that of the people of Plymouth. Moses and the people of Israel are the type; Bradford and the people of Plymouth are the antitype: the journey to America that Bradford and his people make is foreshadowed or prefigured by the journey that Moses and his people make out of Egypt. The land that Moses climbs Pisgah to view is Canaan; the land that Bradford cannot view from a mountain is the American wilderness. But to Bradford and his people, Canaan and America are both one and the same. Through the people of Plymouth, the old and grand drama between God and Satan, between good and evil is re-enacted. Though some of the characters' names are different, the drama is essentially the same.

With the exception of the reference to Moses in the first paragraph, the experiences of the planters are essentially their own experiences and not those of the people of Israel. For example, they cannot find food, inns, houses, friendly natives, mild weather, and a sympathetic captain and crew when they reach Cape Cod. But in the second paragraph, these experiences grow quickly into those of the people of Israel:

> May not and ought not the children of these fathers rightly say: "Our fathers were Eng-

lishmen which came over this great ocean, and were ready to perish in this wilderness; but they cried unto the Lord, and He heard their voice and looked on their adversity," etc. "Let them therefore praise the Lord, because He is good: and His mercies endure forever." "Yea, let them which have been redeemed of the Lord, shew how He hath delivered them from the hand of the oppressor. When they wandered in the desert wilderness out of the way, and found no city to dwell in, both hungry and thirsty, their soul was over-whelmed in them. Let them confess before the Lord his lovingkindness and His wonder-ful works before the sons of men." (emphasis mine)

Clearly, the whole biblical exodus is being re-enacted here. The wandering in the "desert wilder-ness" and the finding of "no city to dwell in" recall Israel's exile and the search for Canaan, the promised land. Reliving the lives of Old and New Testament figures, the planters are, as Rosen-meier has said, "God's living synecdoches," who are paving the way for the new England, the New Jeru-salem, the reformed church, the millennium.[8]

Rosenmeier's study of typology in Of Plymouth Plantation relates typology to the book's structure better than any study with which I am familiar. The book's structure, he contends, emerges from Bradford's frequent perception of events as anal-ogous to Christ's death and resurrection.[9] This observation is difficult to dispute because it is supported by practically every paragraph in the history. But since the Puritans understood typol-ogy as a means of making sense out of everything (e.g., history, the Bible, God), one could add that the structure which grows out of the typology in these two paragraphs is, once again, a movement toward God. For by helping the Puritan understand God, typology brings him closer to Him, the real destination of the parallel epic journeys in both paragraphs.

VI

We saw in section IV how word repetition acted primarily as a device of unity and coherence. The sound patterns in both paragraphs serve an identical function, and alliteration and assonance clearly predominate. Note, for example, how many words in both paragraphs have an initial /s/ sound:

1. stay, stand, so, same
2. sea, seek, succour
3. Scripture, savage, sides
4. season, subject, storms, search
5. see
6. soever, save, solace
7. summer, stand, savage
8. separate, civil
9. said, succour
10. speed, some, season, such, stir, safe, sufficient
11. some
12. supply, succour, sad, small
13. stood
1. sustain, Spirit
2. say
5. city, soul
6. sons

Though Bradford probably was not fully conscious of this intricate sound pattern, there is a clear progression from "stay" (sentence 1, paragraph 1) through "sustain" and "Spirit" (sentence 1, paragraph 2) to "soul" and "sons of men" (sentences 5 and 6, paragraph 2).

Now consider the number of words that begin with a /w/ sound:

1. will
2. well, went, welcome, weatherbeaten
3. with, will, were
4. was, winter, winters
5. wilderness, wild, wild
6. were, wilderness, way

```
 7.  with, weatherbeaten, woods, wild
 8.  was, was, world
10.  with, with, would, was, would, was,
     would, without, would
11.  was, would
12.  weak, were
13.  was
 2.  were, wilderness
 5.  wandered, wilderness, way
 6.  wonderful works
```

There is a clear progression from "will" (sentence 1, paragraph 1) through "wilderness" (sentences 5 and 6, paragraph 1; sentences 2 and 5, paragraph 2) to "wonderful works" of God (sentence 6, paragraph 2).

There is also a pattern that results from a similarity of vowel sounds in the stressed syllables. For instance, there is the /e/ sound:

```
 1.  stay, make, amazed
 2.  preparation, may
 6.  save
 7.  face
10.  place, safe, apace
11.  place
13.  case
 1.  grace
 2.  may, say
```

or the /i/ sound:

```
 1.  people, reader, he
 2.  Being, sea, seek, weatherbeaten
 3.  these
 4.  season, be
 5.  sea, beasts, be
 6.  Neither, feed
 7.  weatherbeaten
 9.  be
10.  speed, be, season, he, be, he, he, keep
11.  leave
12.  be, weak, be
13.  indeed
 3.  he
```

and the /o/ sound:

1. so
2. ocean, before, before, no, no
3. showed, no, arrows
4. know, know, more, coast
6. go, hopes
7. whole
8. ocean
10. go
11. ashore
12. also, hopes
2. over
5. no, both, soul
5. before, before

Interestingly enough, the words that surface in
sentence 6, paragraph 1 as a result of alliteration
and assonance indicate further why this is such a
significant sentence: "save" and "solace"; "were,"
"wilderness," and "way"; "neither" and "feed"; and
"go" and "hopes." These words are practically a
synopsis of both paragraphs. Sound patterns tie
these paragraphs together in a manner that is
simply remarkable.

VII

The repetition of balanced and parallel syntactic patterns also gives unity and coherence to
the paragraphs, as well as a very distinctive
rhythm. There is, for instance, a noticeable pre-
ference for infinitives and infinitive phrases.
The balanced and parallel infinitive phrases in
sentence 2, paragraph 1: "no friends to welcome
them nor inns to entertain or refresh their weatherbeaten bodies, no houses or much less towns to
repair to, to seek for succour" recur in sentence 3
("to fill their sides"), in sentence 4 ("know them
to be sharp and violent, and subject to cruel and
fierce storms, dangerous to travel to known places,
much more to search an unknown coast"), in sentence
6 ("to view from this wilderness" and "to feed
their hopes"), in sentence 8 ("to separate them"),
in sentence 9 ("to succour them"), in sentence 13

("to help them or themselves"), in sentence 2, paragraph 2 ("to perish in this wilderness"), and in sentence 5 ("to dwell in").

The antithetic structure of sentence 2, paragraph 1:

> It is recorded in Scripture as a mercy to the Apostle and his shipwrecked company, that the barbarians showed them no small kindness in refreshing them, but these savage barbarians, when they met with them (as after will appear) were readier to fill their sides full of arrows than otherwise

appears again to some extent in the latter part of sentence 4--"dangerous to travel to known places, much more to search an unknown coast"--and in sentence 9: "If it be said they had a ship to succour them, it is true; but what heard they daily from the master and company?" The if-then syllogistic structure of sentence 9 occurs both in sentence 8--"If they looked behind them, there was the mighty ocean"--and in sentence 11: "Yea, it was muttered by some that if they got not a place in time, they would turn them and their goods ashore and leave them."

Three sentences are in the imperative mood: sentence 12, paragraph 1 ("Let it also be considered. . . ."); sentence 3, paragraph 2 ("Let them therefore praise the Lord. . . ."); and sentence 4 ("Yea, let them which have been redeemed of the Lord").

Although not as systematic as other techniques of balance, there is a tendency in some sentences to balance the number of words before and after semicolons. Sentence 6, paragraph 1, typifies this:

> Neither could they, as it were, go up to the top of Pisgah to view from this wilderness a more goodly country to feed their hopes; for which way soever they turned their eyes (save

upward to the heavens) they could have little solace or content in respect of any outward objects.

There are exactly 26 words preceding the semicolon and 26 following it, perhaps one additional reason why this sentence seems to draw attention to itself.

If for no other reason, these paragraphs achieve balance and parallelism through the use of connectives. Both intrasentence and intersentence connectives are usually preceded and followed by structures of similar grammatical shape.

VIII

Parallel to the paragraph movement or progression that stems from the use of binary stress groups, connectives, couplings, and typology is the movement from the visible to the invisible and back ack to the visible world. Sentence 1, paragraph 1 depicts the visible world. Bradford asks the reader to pause and ponder over the dire predicament of the planters. At this point, theirs is essentially a plight that is visible--that can be seen. But the metaphorical "sea of troubles" in sentence 2 shifts the emphasis to things which are basically unseen. The inability to see--to comprehend--is implicit in the very nature of metaphor: metaphor compares the familiar with the unfamiliar, the concrete with the abstract so that the unfamiliar and the abstract can be better understood. In essence, this is what Bradford does when he compares the Pilgrims' troubles to a sea. And it is at this point that we realize that "this poor peoples's present predicament" is not as simple and clear as sentence 1 would have us believe.

What follows the "sea of troubles" metaphor, then, is invisiblility, because many things are denied to the Pilgrims. When they reach Cape Cod, they find neither "friends," "inns," "houses," nor "towns to repair to, to seek for sucour." They are not given the friendly reception that the natives

59

of Malta give Paul. Instead, the Indians greet them with hostility, ready "to fill their sides full of arrows than otherwise." The weather is "cruel and fierce," making it difficult "to search an <u>unknown</u> coast" (emphasis mine). They know the wilderness is "full of wild beasts and wild men," but they are unable to discern "what multitudes there might be of them." The Pilgrims do not have the advantage or opportunity that Moses had; they cannot climb to the top of a mountain to gain a better conception of the nature of the country and its natives. All "outward objects" are simply difficult to perceive. The complexity of their situation and of the wilderness restricts their vision: "the whole country" is " full of woods and thickets."

The fact that they are isolated compounds their difficulties. The "mighty ocean which they had passed" acts "now as a main bar and gulf," separating them from England and, at the same time, denying them the comfort and assurance that come with the perception of the familiar. Their predicament seems the epitome of isolation: they are separated from "all the civil parts of the world" and not just England. Their ship becomes less and less a real object of aid; the "master and company," frustrated over the increasing difficulty of finding a safe harbor, threaten to abandon them. Indeed, the Pilgrims seem perplexed by it all, and the intricate agreements made with the "merchants at their coming away" do little to facilitate understanding.

But in paragraph 2, all complexities and difficulties succumb to the sustaining power of the "Spirit of God and His grace." There is a clear biblical precedent which gives meaning and order to their plight. They no longer need "to go up to the top of Pisgah"; they can now hear and see through God: "'He heard their voice and looked on their adversity.'" What was once "a hideous and desolate wilderness," "full of woods and thickets," becomes now the visible and "wonderful works" of God.

60

IX

The final significant structural principle (and I add quickly that I make no claim to having discovered them all) that emerges from both paragraphs results from whether the Pilgrims are subjects or objects in sentences. Roughly speaking, in paragraph 1 the Pilgrims are the objects 20 times and subjects 15 times. But even when they are subjects of sentences, they are frequently subjects in dependent clauses (see, for example, sentences 2, 8, 9, 10 and 11). Hence, even when they seem to be in control--to be acting on something else, their actions are nullified by the atmosphere of dependency that stems from the dependent clauses.

From sentences 1-6, they are subjects and objects approximately the same number of times. But sentence 7 erases all doubt about their real predicament: "For summer being done, all things stood upon them with a weatherbeaten face, and the whole country, full of woods and thickets, represented a wild and savage hue" (emphasis mine). The earlier reference to the Pilgrims' "weatherbeaten bodies" in sentence 2 is picked up by the beautifully personified "weatherbeaten face" of "all things." All things--the vast ocean; the sea of troubles; the inability to find friends, inns, and refreshment; the inabiliity to establish friendly relations with the natives; the inability to see through woods and thickets--stand or act upon them. The total image is one of chaos; misfortune rapidly follows misfortune. Simply put, the planters are not in control; they are receivers rather than doers, as the use of the passive voice in sentence 10 ("a safe harbor was discovered by them") and in sentence 11 ("it was muttered by some") indicates further.

In paragraph 2, sentence 1, they occupy the objective slot too, but with a significant difference: "What could now sustain them but the Spirit of God and His grace?" They are now acted upon by God, and that is the way it should be. All

61

their problems disappear. Through God, their sense
of speech becomes functional again: "'He heard
their voice.'" Through Him, their sense of sight
is restored: "'He looked on their adversity.'"
All of this gives rise to a structural principle
that is characterized by a movement from being
acted upon by all "outward objects," and "all
things" to being acted upon by the sustaining power
of God.

    At the intersentence level, it becomes in-
creasingly clear that there are stylistic devices
which promote unity and coherence, yet are repeated
so systematically that they grow into a larger
pattern of structure and meaning. What results is
a multiplicity of reinforcing structural patterns:
(1) the repetition of binary stress groups, (2) the
repetition of connectives and the concept of
alternatives, choice, and possiblity that is shaped
by the connectives, especially the alternative
ones, (3) the repetition of the couplings (as we
have seen, these too are related to choice), (4)
the use of biblical analogy (typology), (5) the
movement from the visible to the invisible and back
to the visible world, and (6) the shifting of the
Pilgrims back and forth from the nominative to the
objective slot. And there are stylistic devices
which work primarily to make the patterns of
structure and meaning unified and coherent, although they too contribute to meaning by causing
key words and phrases to be emphasized: (1) the
use of recurrent sound patterns: alliteration and
assonance, (2) the use of balance and parallelism,
and (3) the use of word or phrase repetition and
synonyms. In short, repetition of various kinds is
the key to structure and meaning in these passages
and, as I hope to prove, the key to the entire
book.

Notes to Chapter 2

[1]In addition to the essays already cited
in the notes to chapter 1, see also Michael Kraus'
The Writing of American History (Norman, Okla.:
University of Oklahoma Press, 1953); Bradford
Smith's Bradford of Plymouth (Philadelphia:
Lippincott, 1951); William Scheick's "The Theme
of Necessity in Bradford's Of Plymouth Plantation,"
Seventeenth-Century News, 32, No. 4 (1974), 88-90;
and Kenneth Alan Hovey's "The Theology of History
in Of Plymouth Plantation and Its Predecessors,"
Early American Literature, 10, No. 1 (1975),
47-66.

[2]See Marckwardt's American English.

[3]The Movement of English Prose, p. 114.

[4]Milic, p. 254.

[5]Contemporary Essays on Style, pp. 21-22.

[6]Since pronoun antecedents are standard
methods of achieving unity and coherence, I have
ignored them.

[7]The Design of the Present, p. 40.

[8]Rosenmeier, p. 104.

[9]Ibid., p. 99.

Chapter 3

Collocation

Appendices are provided at the end of this chapter for each paragraph. Each appendix reflects the surface manifestations of various deep structure constituents and even of various transformations. Appendix I lists all the surface noun phrases of the first paragraph; appendix II provides the collocation of the noun phrases; appendix III lists all the surface verbs and verbals; and appendix IV provides the collocation of the verbs and verbals.

Appendix II suggests that all of the noun phrases tend to group themselves around three nodal items: voyage, sea of troubles, and Lord. These nodal items were not selected arbitrarily. Rather, they were selected because they carry the central concerns of paragraph 1 and confirm the structural movement spoken of earlier, that is, the progression toward God.

Because of the complexity of Bradford's prose --the use of a number of reinforcing unifying and structural principles simultaneously--these nodal items are not totally exclusive of one another; they share part of their collocational range, or have a collocational overlap: some words occur beneath more than one item. But under the nodal item voyage are primarily those words which are specifically related to a voyage or journey. Thus, there are words which indicate the members of the journey: "I" (the narrator), "reader" (especially "the children of these fathers" in paragraph 2), and "they" (the rest of the planters); words which suggest preparation for the voyage: "their preparation," "victuals," and "their goods"; words which tell the means of travel: "vast ocean" and "a ship"; words which relate the seasons: "summer" and "winter"; words which suggest a need for the use of physical and mental abilities: "eyes" and "their minds"; words which reveal a concern for time and distance: "all the civil parts of the world," "speed," "near distance," "a place in time," "their brethren at Leyden," and "their coming away"; words which suggest a captain and crew: "master and company"; words which indicate the sponsors of the voyage: "merchants"; and words which indicate the destination: "country," "known places," "unknown coast," "outward objects," "a place," and "a safe harbor."

With the nodal item sea of troubles, the emphasis is on those words that depict the diffi- culties and complexities that greeted the Pilgrims upon their arrival: "no friends," "no houses," "barbarians," "arrows," "winter," "cruel and fierce storms," "unknown coast," "a hideous and desolate wilderness," "wild beasts and wild men," "all things," "weatherbeaten face," "they" (that is, the Pilgrims themselves), "main bar and gulf," "dan- ger," "weak hopes of supply and succour," "sad condition and trials," "little power," "the case," and the "merchants."

Under the nodal item Lord are those words that are easily associated with the conception of the sustaining God discussed previously. Though they take on different connotations when associated with lord, some of the same words appear that were collocates of voyage and sea of troubles: "suc- cour," "Scripture," "mercy," "Apostle," "top," "Pisgah," "their hopes," "eyes," "heavens," "a safe harbor," "victuals," "their goods," "their minds," and "affections and love." Consequently, two observations should be made at this point. First, the fact that collocates are shared implies that there are connotative levels operating in Bradford's prose. Second, the movement from the general collocate "poor people's present condition" of sea of troubles through all specific collocates of sea of troubles makes clearer my earlier asser- tion that the first paragraph operated mainly by the deductive process.

The collocation of verbs and verbals in paragraph 1 (appendix IV) is quite revealing and brings one closer to meaning and structure. The verbs tend to collocate around five nodal items: verbs of seeing, verbs of tasting, verbs of hearing, verbs of feeling, and verbs of being. Verbs of seeing includes all those verbs that are either clearly related to visual perception or lead to visual perception: "think," "well considers," "went before," "to welcome," "to seek," "showed," "met," "will appear," "know," "to travel," "to search," "knew not," "could . . . go up," "to view," "look," "discovered," etc. Verbs of tasting contains all verbs that are related to food: "to refresh," "to feed," "to succour," and "consumed." Verbs of hearing includes verbs that are explicitly connected with hearing or imply it as a resulting action: "heard," "muttered," and "declared." Verbs of feeling includes verbs that imply some contact between either a man-made object or natural force and the body: "to fill their sides full of arrows," "to be sharp and violent" (that is, the weather), "to be subject to cruel and fierce storms," and "stand upon them." Verbs of being includes all uses of be as a main verb: "was," "were," "is," "would be," "might be," etc.

Clearly, the collocation of the verbs exposes the heart of the paragraph. As Alan Howard has said, "complexity, not Satan, is the real antagonist in the drama of <u>Plymouth Plantation</u>."[1] It is a complexity that requires the use of almost all senses; it is a complexity that results from the uncertainty of one's being, of one's existence. But, as the lengthy number of collocates of verbs of seeing and verbs of being testifies, the major difficulty is one of seeing or perceiving--perceiving "outward objects," as well as one's own being. On a voyage (and note that the notion of a journey is carried mainly by collocates of verbs of seeing: to see, to travel, to search, looked, discovered, etc.) which is at once toward America and God, how does one see into his own heart, the heart of his companions, and the heart of a hostile enemy (which can be himself, the Indians, his companions, or the weather)? How does one see into the invisible? What real alternatives does one have? Can one rely on his own strength or the strength of other men? These are the questions raised by the collocation of nouns and verbs. Even with the exceptional abilities of a few rare men like Bradford, Robinson, and Brewster, there is only one answer. And as we have seen here and above, that answer gives rise to meaning and structure.

The nodal items voyage, sea of troubles, and Lord also serve easily as nodal items in the collocation of noun phrases in paragraph 2 (appendix VI). Voyage includes such collocates as "our fathers," "Englishmen," "great ocean," "the way," and "men." Sea of troubles contains words like "wilderness," "their adversity," "the hand of the oppressor," and "their soul" (hungry and thirsty). Since it clearly dominates this paragraph, the word Lord could easily contain all words, but words of particular note are "Spirit of God and His grace," "Lord (which occurs four times), "He" (which appears three times), "their voice," "His mercies," "the way," "His lovingkindness," "His wonderful works," "sons," and "men."

Sea of troubles does not represent the same type of difficulties as was seen in paragraph 1. In paragraph 1, the Pilgrims see, hear, and taste their troubles; they are immediate. But the troubles in paragraph 2 are rhetorical; they are types which are designed to assist the Pilgrims in selecting alternatives. There is in paragraph 2 the sense of a resolution that is not in paragraph 1. The people of Israel have reached their destination and realized God's plan; He has shown them the way.

This same idea of resolution is picked up by the collocation of the verbs in paragraph 2 (appendix VIII). The verbs group around four nodal items: verbs of sustaining, verbs of seeing, verbs of hearing, and verbs of being. The verbs of sustaining control the paragraph: "could now sustain," "endure forever, " "redeemed," and "hath delivered." Although there are verbs of seeing ("looked," "shew," and "found") and verbs of hearing ("cried" and "heard), it is God who is seeing and hearing, leading "the way." There are few verbs of being because the Pilgrims have discovered themselves through analogy.

Though all structural movements progress toward God, we can now say that collocation has enabled us to refine some structural principles and to discover some additional ones that were not so apparent before. First, it is clearer now that the voyage is a multiple one which must choose God as the destination. On this voyage, one discovers the self and other men. Perhaps the most important passenger on the Mayflower is the reader. As Rosenmeier has said, the Pilgrims serve more as synecdoches than as antitypes, paving the way for the millennium. As the people of Israel served as examples for the Pilgrims, the Pilgrims now serve as examples for the reader. And that reader is none other than the "children of these fathers" in paragraph 2. Therefore, the "reader" of paragaph 1 moves rapidly toward specification, toward the "children of these fathers."

The relationship between "the reader" and "the children of these fathers" introduces a second structural refinement: almost every noun and verb in paragraph 1 has a postcedent in paragraph 2, which sometimes has a similar or the same phono-logical shape. For example, consider the following scheme:

Paragraph 1	Paragraph 2
vast ocean	great ocean
no towns	no city
mercy	His mercies
barbarians	
arrow	
season	
winter	
cruel and fierce storms	
woods and thickets	
the merchants	the hand of the opppressor
succour	

```
their hopes
eyes     ´
heavens                  Lord
to succour                  could now sustain
hath . . . declared      rightly say
to travel
to search
to seek                  came over
show                     shew
looked                   looked
```

One could continue this list with little difficulty, but this should be sufficient to demonstrate
the close parallel between nouns and verbs in both
paragraphs. If nothing else, this scheme confirms
an earlier observation that the second paragraph
functions much like a concluding sentence. On the
one hand, it summarizes because the experiences of
the people of Israel and Plymouth are one and the
same; on the other hand, it expands because it is
analogical, encompassing two experiences to make
them one.

        Collocation also makes more apparent two
additional structural patterns. First, a negative-
positive relationship exists between the two
paragraphs. The negative verbs of paragraph 1
("cannot," "knew not," "would not stir," "got not,"
"could not . . . be," and many others that are
negative in connotation) yield to the positive
verbs of paragraph 2 ("could now sustain," "endure
forever," "praise," "have been redeemed," "hath
delivered," and "confess"). To a certain extent,
this is true of the nouns. Simply put, the whole
of paragraph 1 is negative in connotation and that
of paragraph 2 is positive, as it should be since
God is central to it.

        Second, collocation reveals a structural
pattern that functions mainly by connotation.
There is a noticeable progression from the earthly
food which quiets the appetite and nourishes the
body of paragraph 1 to the heavenly food which
feeds the "hungry and thirsty" soul of paragraph
2. Many references are made to food or eating in

paragraph 1: "refresh," "refreshing," "to feed their hopes," "victuals consumed," and "supply and succour." These references culminate in paragraph 2: "sustain" and "hungry and thirsty" soul. Feeding of the soul is what the Pilgrims should have been concerned with from the very beginning. Since only God can supply this type of food, the Pilgrims are reminded once again that God (and all of His manifestations) is the only enduring alternative.

Appendix I

Noun Phrases, Paragraph 1

1. I
    a pause
    this poor people's
       present condition
    I
    the reader
    he
    the same

2. the vast ocean
    a sea of troubles
    their preparation
    they
    no friends
    them
    (no) inns
    their weatherbeaten
       bodies
    no houses
    (no) towns
    succour

3. It
    Scripture
    mercy
    Apostle
    his shipwrecked
       company
    the barbarians
    them
    no small kindness
    these savage
       barbarians
    them
    they
    their sides
    arrows

4. season
    it

winter
they
the winters
that country
them
cruel and fierce
   storms
known places
unknown coast

5. what
    they
    a hideous and
       desolate
       wilderness
    wild beasts and
       wild men
    multitudes
    them
    they

6. they
    it
    the top
    Pisgah
    this wilderness
    a more goodly
       country
    their hopes
    they
    their eyes
    the heavens
    they
    little solace or
       content
    any outward
       objects

7. summer
    all things

them
a weatherbeaten
  face
the whole country
woods and thickets
a wild and savage
  hue

8. them
they
the mighty ocean
a main bar and gulf
all the civil parts
  of the world

9. it
they
a ship
them
it
what
they
the master and
  company

10. speed
they
a place
their shallop
they
some near distance
the season
he
a safe harbor
them
they
he
danger
victuals
he
their return

11. it
some
they
a place in time
they
them
their goods

12. weak hopes of
  supply and
  succour
them
this sad condition
  and trials
they
they
very small

13. It
the affections and
  love
their brethren at
  Leyden
them
they
little power
the case
them
the merchants
their coming away

Appendix II

Collocation of Noun Phrases, Paragraph 1

Nodal
Items: <u>Voyage</u>

1. I
    a pause
    the reader
    he

2. the vast ocean
    their preparation
    they
    their weather-
        beaten bodies

3. his shipwrecked
        company

4. season
    winter
    the winters
    that country
    cruel and
        fierce storms
    known places
    unknown coast

5. they

6. they
    top
    Pisgah
    their eyes
    any outward
        objects

7. all things
    them
    a weatherbeaten
        face
    the whole country

8. the mighty ocean
    they
    all the civil parts
        of the world

9. a ship
    the master and
        company

10. speed
    they
    a place
    their shallop
    some near distance
    the season
    he
    a safe harbor
    them
    danger
    victuals
    their return

11. some
    they
    a place in time
    their goods

12. weak hopes
    they
    their minds
    sad condition and
        trials
    they

Nodal
Item: Voyage

13. affections and
       love
    their brethren
    at Leyden
    they
    little power
    the case
    merchants
    their coming away

Nodal
Item: Sea of Troubles

1. Poor people's
      present con-
      dition

2. vast ocean
   their preparation
   no friends
   inns
   their weather-
      beaten bodies
   no houses
   (no) towns

3. the barbarians
   them
   no small kindness
   these savage
      barbarians
   them
   their sides
   arrows

4. winter
   winters
   country

   them
   cruel and fierce
      storms
   unknown coast

5. they
   a hideous and
      desolate
      wilderness
   wild beasts and
      wild men
   multitudes
   they

6. they
   this wilderness
   little solace or
      content

7. all things
   weatherbeaten face
   woods and thickets
   wild and savage hue

8. they
   mighty ocean
   main bar and gulf

9. a ship
   master and company

10. they
    a place
    season
    he
    danger

Appendix II continued

Nodal
Item: Sea of Troubles

11.   they   12. their minds
      a place in time   trials
      them
                            13. affections
12.   weak hopes of   and love
        supply and
        succour
      their minds
      this sad condition
        and trials
      they

13.   their brethren
        at Leyden
      them
      little power
      the case
      the merchants
      their coming away

Nodal
Item: Lord

 1.   succour

 3.   Scripture
      mercy
      Apostle

 6.   the top
      Pisgah
      their hopes
      their eyes
      the heavens

10.   a safe harbor

11.   their goods

Appendix III

Verbs and Verbals--Paragraph I

1. cannot
    stay
    make
    stand half amazed
    think
    will
    well considers

2. Being thus passed
    may be remembered
    went before
    had
    to welcome
    to entertain or
      refresh
    to repair to
    to seek

3. is recorded
    showed
    met
    will appear
    were
    to fill

4. was
    know
    know
    to be sharp and
      violent
    (to be) subject
    to travel
    to search

5. see
    might be
    knew not

6. were
    could . . . go up
    to view

    to feed
    turn
    could have

7. stand
    represented

8. looked
    was
    had passed
    was now
    to separate

9. be said
    had
    to succour
    is
    heard

10. should look out
    would be
    was
    would not stir
    was discovered
    would be
    might go
    consumed apace
    must and would
      keep

11. was muttered
    got not
    would turn
    leave

12. Let
    be considered
    left behind
    might bear up
    were under. . .
    could not . . . be

76

13.   is
      was
      had
      to help
      stood
      hath already been
        declared

Collocation of Verbs and Verbals--Paragraph 1

Nodal Item: **Verbs of Seeing**	Nodal Item: **Verbs of Tasting**
1. stand half amazed think well considers	2. to refresh
	6. to feed
2. went before to welcome to entertain to seek	9. to succour
	10. consumed
3. showed met will appear	Nodal Item: **Verbs of Hearing**
	9. heard
4. know to travel to search	10. was muttered
	11. declared
5. to see knew not	Nodal Item: **Verbs of Being**
6. could . . . go up to view turn	3. were
	4. was
7. represent	5. might be
8. looked had passed to separate	6. were
	8. was was now
10. should look out discovered	9. is
12. be considered left behind	10. would be was

Nodal
Item: Verbs of Being

12.   were under
      could not be

13.   is
      was

Nodal
Item: Verbs of Feeling

 3.   to fill (their sides
      full of arrows

 4.   to be sharp and
      violent
      (to be) subject to
      cruel and fierce
      storms

 7.   stand (upon them)

Noun Phrases, Paragraph 2

1. them
   the Spirit of God and His grace

2. the children of these fathers
   our fathers
   Englishmen
   this great ocean
   this wilderness
   they
   the Lord
   He
   their voice
   their adversity

3. them
   Lord
   He
   His mercies

4. them
   Lord
   He
   them
   the hand of the oppressor

5. they
   the desert wilderness
   the way
   no city
   their soul (hungry and thirsty)

6. them
   Lord
   His lovingkindness
   His wonderful works
   the sons
   men

Appendix VI

Collocation of Noun Phrases, Paragraph 2

Nodal
Item: Voyage

2. our fathers
    Englishmen
    this great ocean
    they

5. the way

6. the sons
    men

Nodal
Item: Sea of Troubles

2. this wilderness
    their adversity
    the hand of the
       oppressor

5. the desert
       wilderness
    no city
    their soul
       (hungry and
       thirsty)

Nodal
Item: Lord

1. Spirit of God and
       His grace

2. Lord
    He
    their voice

3. Lord
    He
    His mercies

4. Lord
    He

5. the way
    their soul

6. Lord
    His loving-
       kindness
    His wonderful
       works
    the sons
    men

Verbs and Verbals--Paragraph 2

1. could now sustain

2. may not and ought not
   rightly say
   were
   came over
   were ready
   to perish
   cried
   heard
   looked

3. let
   praise
   is
   endure forever

4. let
   have been redeemed
   shew
   hath delivered

5. wandered
   found
   to dwell in
   was overwhelmed

6. confess

Appendix VIII

Collocation of Verbs and Verbals--Paragraph 2

Nodal
Item: <u>Verbs of Sustaining</u>

1. could now sustain

3. praise
   endure forever

4. redeemed
   hath delivered

6. confess

Nodal
Item: <u>Verbs of Seeing</u>

2. looked

4. shew

5. found

Nodal
Item: <u>Verbs of Hearing</u>

2. cried
   heard

Nodal
Item: <u>Verbs of Being</u>

2. were
   were ready

3. is

5. was

[1] "Art and History in Bradford's _Of Plymouth Plantation_," _William and Mary Quarterly_, 28 (1971), 249.

Chapter 4

A Discussion of Other Paragraphs

If the foregrounded passages are truly representative, then one should find many of the same stylistic devices which gave them unity, coherence, meaning, and structure doing essentially the same thing for other passages. Again, these stylistic devices are of two types--those which contribute to unity and coherence, yet are repeated so systematically or are such an integral part of the paragraphs that they grow into larger patterns of structure and meaning: (1) the repetition of binary stress groups, (2) the repetition of the couplings, (3) the repetition of connectives, (4) the use of biblical analogy, (5) the movement from the visible to the invisible and back to the visible world, (6) the shifting of the Pilgrims back and forth from subjects to objects, (7) the movement from the negative to the positive, and (8) the movement from the feeding of the body to the feeding of the soul. Then, there are those which work primarily to make the patterns of structure and meaning unified and coherent, although they too contribute to meaning by emphasizing key words and phrases: (1) the use of alliteration and assonance, (2) the use of balance and parallelism, and (3) the use of word or phrase repetition and synonyms. What should be stressed here, especially about the structural patterns, is that they all reinforce one another; they all move toward God. In some paragraphs, we will find structural patterns in the same form as they have occurred above. In others, we will find only a major part of the structural patterns. Some structural patterns we may not see again, e.g., the movement from the feeding of the body to the feeding of the soul. Still, there are others that we may see only small parts of, e.g., the shifting of the Pilgrims back and forth from the nominative to the objective slot. But this should be expected. The foregrounded paragraphs are representative, not perfectly identical to every other paragraph in the history.

85

Since a major assumption of this study is that the individual episode is far more significant than cause and effect or chronological relations, the selection of other passages presents few problems. What I have tried to do is select passages near the beginning, middle, and end of the history. Although certainly not in the same detail and depth as in the preceding chapters, the remainder of this chapter will analyze other passages in the history, showing how their stylistic features evolve from those of the foregrounded paragraphs. For each paragraph, I will discuss the devices of structure and meaning first, and the devices of unity and coherence second, following the same order as indicated in the summary of stylistic devices above.

The first paragraph is the first paragraph in the history:

> It is well known unto the godly and judicious, how ever since the first breaking out of the light of the gospel in our honourable nation of England, (which was the first of nations whom the Lord adorned therewith after the gross darkness of popery which had covered and overspread the Christian world), what wars and oppositions ever since, Satan hath raised, maintained and continued against the Saints, from time to time, in one sort or other. Sometimes by bloody death and cruel torments; other whiles imprisonments, banishments and other hard usages; as being loath his kingdom should go down, the truth prevail and the churches of God revert to their ancient purity and recover their primitive order, liberty and beauty. (p. 3)

Sentence 1 divides into stress groups of 5, 6, 3, 7, 4, 5, 3, 2, 2, 2, 2, and 2:

/ u ` / u / u / u u/u
It is well known unto the godly and judicious,

/ u / ᴜ ` / ᴜ / ᴜ
/ how ever since the first breaking out of

86

the light of the gospel / in our honourable

nation of England, / (which was the first of

nations whom the Lord adorned therewith

,' after the gross darkness of popery / which

had covered and overspread the Christian

world, / what wars and oppositions ever since,

/ Satan hath raised, / maintained and con

tinued ,' against the Saints, / from time to

time, / in one sort or other.

Though it occurs in a five-stress group, the coupling "godly and judicious" quietly and subtly announces the two beat rythm. The sentence then rushes through numerous couplings to a five consecutive binary stress group conclusion.

Sentence 2 divides into stress groups of 3, 3, 2, 3, 2, 2, 3, 3, and 2:

Sometimes by bloody death and cruel torments;

/ other whiles imprisonments, / banishments

and other hard usages; / as being loath his

kingdom should go down, / the truth prevail

,' and the churches of God ,' revert to their

ancient purity ,' and recover their primitive

order, / liberty and beauty.

Nowhere are the various effects of the couplings on rhythm clearer than in sentence 2. The couplings, it seems to me, almost insist that they receive the greatest emphasis, no matter where and in what form they appear. For instance, the nouns in the coupling "bloody death and cruel torments" take the emphasis away from the adjectives, causing them to distribute their stresses. The same thing occurs in the latter part of "banishments and other hard usages." The result of all this is a consistent two beat rhythm that marches grandly toward "the churches of God."

The couplings are inseparable from stress groups--from rhythm. And since the discussion of stress groups has shown that the couplings are present, all that remains now is to indicate that they occur frequently enough to grow into a structural principle: "godly and judicious," "covered and overspread," "wars and oppositions," "bloody death and cruel torments," "banishments and other hard usages," and to a lesser extent, "liberty and beauty." Little more need be said.

While this paragraph is not as extensively connected as the foregrounded passages, it is very much concerned with the notion of choice and possibility. In the eternal war which Satan wages against the saints, he has defeated them on almost all fronts, exhausted practically all of their alternatives. He has attacked them through "the gross darkness of popery"; he has "raised, maintained and continued" wars and oppositions against them; he has used "bloody death and cruel torments," "imprisonments, banishments" and the like in an effort to conquer them. Therefore, as the couplings and paragraph movement suggest, the saints have only one choice or alternative left: to 2revert to the ancient purity" of "the churches of God."

Biblical analogy is also a major structural principle. While the analogy is not rooted in a specific reference to a biblical type, it is present in the imagery--in the rise and fall movement--in the similarity between the history of Pilgrim suffering and Christ's passion, as Rosenmeier has pointed out so adeptly.[1] The "gross darkness of popery," Satan's "wars and

oppositions," his "bloody death and cruel torments," "imprisonments, banishments and other hard
usages"--all of these culminate in the verb phrase
"go down." But the saints are able to offset this
declining or falling movement, are able to regain
their former status through the churches of God,
which "revert to their ancient purity and recover
their primitive order, liberty and beauty" (emphasis mine).

Perhaps the most important structural pattern
is the movement from the visible to the invisible
and back to the visible world. The paragraph
progresses from "the light of the gospel," which
enables things to be seen and comprehended, to the
"gross darkness of popery," where things are
"covered and overspread." This, to be sure, is a
very difficult and complex stage in the saints'
lives. Satan employs a multiplicity of strategems
against them, bringing chaos and confusion into
their lives. However, with the reference to "the
churches of God," the paragraph returns to the
visible world: "purity," "order," "liberty," and
"beauty" are restored. Implicit in this structural
pattern are two additional ones. The first is the
movement from the chaotic world of Satan to the
very ordered world of God. In one sense, then, one
could argue that individual paragraphs and the
history move toward a definition of God. In the
foregrounded passages, God is defined as one who
sustains; here, He is defined as one who provides
order. The second is the movement from the world
of spirit, an immersion in the imbroglio of history, and a return to the world of purity and
spirit as in pre-historical ages: that is, in the
era of primeval Christian fellowship.

At this point in the history, Bradford recounts the sufferings of the planters' ancestors.
But they, like the planters when they reach Cape
Cod, are depicted as people who are acted upon;
they are receivers rather than doers; they are
objects rather than subjects. As was discovered in
the discussion of the foregrounded pararaphs, the
Pilgrims had little control even when they served

as subjects. Thus, what is ultimately of primary
concern to the Pilgrims and their ancestors is the
nature of the force that is acting upon them. In
the first part of this paragraph, the saints are
the recipients of Satan's crafty devices and
schemes. In the latter part of the paragraph, the
saints are acted upon by God. Throughout the
history, it is only when the Pilgrims are acted
upon by God that "truth," "order," "liberty," and
"beauty" prevail. Whenever they are acted upon by
anything or anyone else (and this includes such
godly men as Bradford, Robinson, and Brewster),
chaos seems inevitable.

And finally, as was observed previously in
chapter 3, there is a movement from the negative to
the positive, which is particularly evident in the
progression of the verbs: "is," "was," "adorned,"
"covered," "overspread," "hath raised," "main-
tain," "continued," "should go down," "prevail,"
"revert," and "recover." Furthermore, the nouns
and verbs collocate easily around the nodal items
voyage, sea of troubles, and Lord. Sight words
(e.g., light, darkness) continue to play a major
role.

Alliterative patterns give unity and coherence
to these structural patterns. There are words
which begin with a /g/ sound: "godly," "gospel,"
"gross," "go," and "God"; words which begin with a
/p/ sound: "popery," "prevail," "purity," and
"primitive"; and words which begin with an /s/
sound: "since," "Satan," "Saints," "sort," and
"sometimes," creating an effective serpent-like
sound and image that are so typical of Satan.
Almost unfailingly, alliteration (as well as
assonance) foregrounds pertinent words: "godly,"
"gospel," and "God"; "gross," "popery," "loath,"
and "go."

Word repetition and synonyms do not play as
significant a role as they did in the foregrounded
passages. "First," "since," and "nation" are
repeated twice. "Saints" and "Lord" provide
synonyms or collocates for "godly." Practically

all words that have negative connotations can be considered synonyms or collocates of Satan.

The most remarkable device of unity and coherence is a balanced sentence structure. A perfect, antithetical relationship exists between sentences 1 and 2. "Covered" in sentence 1 contrasts sharply with "recovered" in sentence 2. All of Satan's cruel acts in sentence 1 are undercut by the sustaining and enduring power of the churches of God in sentence 2.

The second paragraph is taken from chapter 2 and concerns the Pilgrims' flight to Holland:

But the poor men which were got aboard were in great distress for their wives and children which they saw thus to be taken, and were left destitute of their helps; and themselves also, not having a cloth to shift them with, more than they had on their backs, and some scarce a penny about them, all they had being aboard the bark. It drew tears from their eyes, and anything they had they would have given to have been ashore again; but all in vain, there was no remedy, they must thus sadly part. And afterward endured a fearful storm at sea, being fourteen days or more before they arrived at their port; in seven whereof they neither saw sun, moon nor stars, and were driven near the coast of Norway; the mariners themselves often despairing of life, and once with shrieks and cries gave over all, as if the ship had been foundered in the sea and they sinking without recovery. But when man's hope and help wholly failed, the Lord's power and mercy appeared in their recovery; for the ship rose again and gave the mariners courage again to manage her. And if modesty would suffer me, I might declare with what fervent prayers they cried unto the Lord in this great distress (especially some of them) even without any great distraction. When the water ran into their mouths and ears and the mariners cried out, "We sink, we sink!" they

cried (if not with miraculous, yet with a
great height or degree of divine faith), "Yet
Lord Thou canst save! Yet Lord Thou canst
save!" with such other expressions as I will
forbear. Upon which the ship did not only
recover, but shortly after the violence of the
storm began to abate, and the Lord filled
their afflicted minds with such comforts as
everyone cannot understand, and in the end
brought them to their desired haven, where the
people came flocking, admiring their deliverance; the storm having been so long and
sore, in which much hurt had been done, as the
master's friends related unto him in their
congratulations. (pp. 13-14)

One only needs to examine half of this paragraph to see how pervasive binary stress groups
are--how the rhythm rises and falls toward God.
Sentence 1 divides into stress groups of 2, 2, 5,
2, 2, 2, 3, 4, 4, and 4:

But the poor men / which were got aboard

/ were in great distress for their wives and

children / which they saw thus to be taken, /

and were left destitute of their helps; / and

themselves also, / not having a cloth to shift

them with, / more than they had on their

backs, / and some scarce a penny about them, /

all they had being aboard the bark.

While not a coupling, "wives and children" has
basically the same relationship to rhythm as the
couplings have because it has the shape of a
coupling. The couplings force the reader to hear
the rhythm in terms of two's. It is mainly this
insistent and consistent two beat rhythm that
causes Bradford's prose to abound in distributed

stresses, as in the fourth and fifth foot-divisions
for example. As usual, five and three four-stress
groups give variety to a rhythm that otherwise
would be extremely monotonous.

Sentence 2 divides into stress groups of 2, 2,
5, 2, 2, and 3:

It drew tears from their eyes, / and anything
they had / they would have given to have been
ashore again; / but all in vain, / there was
no remedy, / they must thus sadly part.

Sentence 3 consists of stress groups of 5, 7, 2, 5,
4, 5, 3, 2, 3, 2, and 2:

And afterward endured a fearful storm at sea,
/ being fourteen days or more before they
arrived at their port; / in seven whereof
/they neither saw sun, moon nor stars, / and
were driven near the coast of Norway; / the
mariners themselves often despairing of life,
/ and once with shrieks and cries / gave over
all, / as if the ship had been foundered in
the sea / and they sinking / without recovery.

The two opening rhythmic sequences expand, acting
out the difficulties the Pilgrims face at sea.
Sentence 4 divides into stress groups of 2, 2, 2,
2, 2, 4, and 2:

But when man's hope and help / wholly failed,
/ the Lord's power and mercy / appeared in

their recovery; / for the ship rose again
/ and gave the mariners courage again / to
manage her.

This sentence is just one of many that demonstrates
vividly the relationship between rhythm and the
couplings. "Man's hope and help" is balanced
neatly with "Lord's power and mercy." Both dictate
a two beat rhythm, a rhythm that moves toward the
Lord.

This paragraph also demonstrates clearly the
relationship between the couplings and structure.
Though the couplings do not occur here as frequently as they did in the paragraphs discussed
earlier, they are placed in key positions throughout the paragraph. From the coupling-like "wives
and children" of sentence 1, the couplings move
through "shrieks and cries" of sentence 3, "man's
hope and help" and the "Lord's power and mercy" of
sentence 4, to the "height or degree of divine
faith" of sentence 6. These couplings constitute a
story in themselves. As they progress toward a
"height or degree of divine faith," so do the
Pilgrims.

The extensively connected prose of this
paragraph makes one realize that the argument here
is essentially the same as it was in the foregrounded paragraphs: man has no alternatives or
choices among men. The connectives give the
argument the same persuasiveness, clarity, and form
as they did previously. The notion of choice is
underscored by the alternative connectives (e.g.,
"neither . . . nor" in sentence 3). The "poor men"
aboard ship are crushed by the plight of their
wives and children; they are left without clothes
or money. The men will do or give anything to join
their families again, "but all in vain, there was
no remedy." The men have little or no choice; they
have little or no control of their lives. At sea,
a fearful storm or nature becomes surrogates for
the adventurers as controllers of the Pilgrims'

lives. The storm wrests all sense of direction
from them. "Dispairing of life," they cry out that
all is lost and give "over all," thinking that they
are "sinking without recovery." "But when man's
hope and help wholly failed, the Lord's power and
mercy appeared in their recovery; for the ship rose
again and gave the mariners courage again to manage
her." Once again, God is viewed as the ultimate
alternative and destination. The remainder of this
paragraph, sentences 5-7, is an expansion of this
idea.

The abundant sinking and rising images indicate that biblical analogy is still very much a
structural principle. Prior to this paragraph, the
Pilgrims, like Christ, have been "betrayed" several
times by the mariners in seeking "means of con-
veyance" to Holland. This paragraph recounts this
experience as analogous to Christ's resurrection.
Roughly half of the paragraph depicts experiences
similar to those of Christ before the resurrection;
the rest depicts similar experiences after it. The
image of "sinking without recovery" sums up all the
problems revealed in the first half of the paragraph: the desperate predicament of the wives and
children and the men, the separation of families,
and the fearful storm and the consequent loss of
direction. But when the Lord intervenes with
"power and mercy," the "ship rose again," resur-
recting with it the Pilgrims from a former death-
like plight (emphasis mine).

The movement from the visible to the invisible
and back to the visible world continues to be a
significant structural device. The men see the
"great distress" that their wives and children are
in. Their families are "left destitute of their
helps" with few clothes and little money: "It drew
tears from their eyes." After fourteen days at sea
and at the mercy of a "fearful storm," things
become invisible or at best extremely difficult to
perceive: "they neither saw sun, moon nor stars,
and were driven near the coast of Norway." Sight
is restored however when "the Lord's power and
mercy appeared in their recovery." Since God is

now acting upon them, the mariners regain courage and are able to manage the ship again, as well as their lives. The Lord fills "their afflicted minds with such comforts as everyone cannot understand." As a result, their sense of direction is restored; they can now find "their desired haven," which was all too invisible before.

Collocation reveals that this paragraph, like the ones discussed previously, is very much concerned with a twofold journey toward Holland and God. All nouns and noun phrases are collocates of either voyage, sea of troubles, or Lord. Voyage includes such words as "poor men," "a cloth," "backs," "a penny," "eyes," "port," "sun," "stars," "mariners," "ship," "sea," "courage," modesty," "I," "prayers," "mouth and ears," and "great height and degree of divine faith." The progression of the collocates of voyage is significant. What is suggested is that "poor men" need many things on a voyage. But above all, they need "courage," "modesty," "prayers," and a "great height or degree of divine faith," especially on a voyage toward God. Such, it seems to me, reaches the heart of the history.

Sea of troubles includes such words as "great distress," "tears," "no remedy," "cries," "afflicted minds," and "hurt"; Lord contains "life," "recovery," "man's hope and help," "Lord's power and mercy," "comforts," "end," "their desired haven," and "deliverance." In addition to being a sustainer and provider, God clearly becomes now a life-giving force, a force that recovers and comforts--the "end" and "desired haven" of one's journey.

As a whole, the verbs and verbals are collocates of either verbs of being, verbs of sustaining, or verbs of hearing. As should be expected, the emphasis is on verbs of seeing (saw, appeared, rose, and sink), verbs of hearing (might declare, cried, cried out, and related), and verbs of sustaining (endured, arrived, to manage, save, filled, and brought). But ultimately, the sight words are most important. For the perception of alternatives, of the ways of nature, men, and God is of first importance throughout the history.

The lists of nouns and verbs suggest the presence of a negative-positive movement. By now, it should be fairly evident that this structural pattern is implicit in all others. Anytime there is a movement toward God, there is a parallel movement toward words which are positive in tone. Therefore, this structural pattern will no longer receive separate attention. One should and can accept it as a given that this structural principle is very much a part of the remaining paragraphs to be discussed in this study.

Words that have similar initial sounds give unity and coherence to these structural patterns. Of primary importance are words that have initial /s/ sounds: "saw," "some," "sadly," "sea," "seven," "sinking," "suffer," "save," "such," "so," and "sore; words that have initial /d/ sounds: "distress," "destitute," "driven," "desired," "deliverance," and "done"; words that have initial /p/ sounds: "poor," "penny," "party," "port," "power," "prayers," and "people"; words that have initial /h/ sounds: "helps," "had," "have," "hope," "help," "haven," "hurt," and "him"; and words that have initial /f/ sounds: "fourteen," "foundered," "failed," "fervent," "faith," "forbear," "filled," "flocking," and "friends." Almost without exception, significant words can be grouped according to the similarity in the beginning sound.

Although not to the degree of the alliterative patterns, assonance plays at least a noticeable role: "aboard," "poor," "ashore," "more," and "before"; "coast," "hope," "rose," and "sore"; "taken," "gave," "save," "haven," and "related"; "declare" and "prayers"; and "sea" and "degree."

Yet balance continues to be the leading device of unity and coherence. A perfect, antithetic relationship exists between sentences 1-3 and 4-7. Sentences 1-3 are controlled by the image of sinking. Poor families that have practically no clothing and money are separated. The men encounter a violent storm at sea which wrests all sense of time and direction from them. They feel that they are "sinking without recovery." However, sentence 4 introduces the opposite image of rising: the "Lord appeared in their recovery," and the "ship rose again." This rising imagery is sustained for the remainder of the paragraph.

The repetition of words and the use of synonyms contribute to unity and coherence. "Ship" is repeated three times and is also referred to as a "bark." "Saw" occurs twice, as well as the plentiful words that are related to seeing, such as "eyes." "Recovery" appears twice in the noun form and once as a verb. "Mariner" is repeated twice, as well as "great distress." "Cry" appears four times, once in the present tense and three times in the past. "Sea" occurs twice and is also referred to as "water." "Storm" is repeated three times.

The third couple of paragraphs appears in chapter 15; they tell of the notorious John Lyford. Contrary to his practice in previous passages, Bradford requires many paragraphs before he can come to any kind of a resolution or conclusion about Lyford. Thus, one should not expect to find in the following two paragraphs all structural patterns in their entirety. What one will find instead is a significant part of the structural patterns. As I hope to show, however, if one keeps the whole Lyford episode in mind while examining the following paragraphs, he will find all structural principles completely intact:

The third eminent person (which the letters before mention) was the minister which they sent over, by the name Mr. John Lyford. Of whom and whose doing I must be more large, though I shall abridge things as much as I can. When this man first came ashore, he saluted them with that reverence and humility as is seldom to be seen, and indeed made them ashamed, he so bowed and cringed unto them,

and would have kissed their hands if they
would have suffered him; yea, he wept and shed
many tears, blessing God that had brought him
to see their faces, and admiring the things
they had done in their wants, etc., as if he
had been made all of love and the humblest
person in the world. And all the while (if we
may judged by his after carriages) he was but
like him mentioned in Psalm x.10, "That
croucheth and boweth, that heaps of poor may
fall by his might." Or like to that dissembling Ishmael, who, when he had slain
Gedaliah, went out weeping and met them that
were coming to offer incense in the house of
the Lord, saying "Come to Gedaliah" when he
meant to slay them.

They gave him the best entertainment they
could, in all simplicity, and a larger allow-
ance of food out of the store than any other
had; and as the Governor had used, in all
weighty affairs to consult with their Elder,
Mr. Brewster, together with his assistants, so
now he called Mr. Lyford also to counsel with
them in their weightiest businesses. After
some short time he desired to join himself a
member to the church here, and was accordingly
received. He made a large confession of his
faith, and an acknowledgment of former disorderly walking and his being entangled with
many corruptions, which had been a burthen to
his conscience, and blessed God for this
opportunity of freedom and liberty to enjoy
the ordinances of God in purity among His
people; with many more such like expressions.
(pp. 147-148)

A scansion of the first paragraph demonstrates
sufficiently that binary stress groups continue to
prevail. At this point, it is important that the
reader recall that my scansion of paragraphs is not
necessarily a key to the reading of them. Rather,
I am trying to uncover those symmetrical patterns--
those underlying schemes which are a direct result
of the couplings.

2, 4, 2, 2, and 3 is the pattern of stress groups in sentence 1:

The third eminent person / (which the letters before mention) / was the minister / which they sent over, / by name Mr. John Lyford.

The stress groups in sentence 2 are 3, 3, 2, and 2:

Of whom and whose doing / I must be more large, / though I shall abridge things / as much as I can.

Though it is in a three-stress group, the coupling "whom and whose" and the two stresses it receives is what attracts one's attention. After this, one is simply compelled to search for a rhythm of two's. The stress groups in sentence 3 are 3, 2, 2, 2, 1, 2, 2, 2, 2, 3, 2, 2, 3, 2, 2, 2, 3, 4, 4, and 3:

When this man first came ashore, / he saluted them / with that reverence and humility / as is seldom to be seen, / and indeed / made them ashamed, / he so bowed and cringed / unto them, / and would have kissed their hands / if they would have suffered him; / yea, he wept and shed / many tears, / blessing God / that had brought him to see their faces, / and admiring the things they had done in their

100

wants, etc., / as if he had been made all of love / and the humblest person in the world.

Again, three couplings dictate the rhythm of the sentence. 2, 2, 2, 2, 2, 2, and 4 are the stress groups in sentence 4.

And all the while / (if we may judge / by his after carriages) / he was but like him / mentioned in Psalm x.10, / "That croucheth and boweth, / that heaps of poor may fall by his might."

The quote from Psalms, particularly the coupling it contains, provides additional evidence that the Bible is a major source of Bradford's style, especially his rhythm. The stress groups of the last sentence in paragraph 1 are 3, 1, 3, 2, 3, 2, 3, and 2:

Or like to that dissembling Ishmael, / who, / when he had slain Gedaliah, / went out weeping and met them / that were coming to offer incense / in the house of the Lord, / saying "Come to Gedaliah" / when he meant to slay them.

As was implicit in the discussion of the rhythm, the couplings are plentiful enough to consider them as a structural principle. Paragraph 1 contains five couplings: "whom and whose," "reverence and humility," "bowed and cringed," "wept and shed," and "croucheth and boweth"; paragraph 2 contains one coupling which comes neatly and effectively at the end of the paragraph: "freedom and liberty."

The movement from one alternative to another and finally toward God as the only real alternative begins with these two paragraphs and runs throughout the entire Lyford (and Oldham) episode (pp. 147-169). As before, this movement is underscored by the numerous alternative connectives that occur throughout the episode. The Pilgrims do not know what to make of Lyford. Time after time, he takes advantage of them. He greets them and confesses his sins extravagantly while he simultaneously spreads dissension through "private meetings," "whisperings," and clandestine letters. Confronted with a corrupt minister like Lyford, the Pilgrims have only one alternative. And an acknowledgment of this comes early: "God only knows" (p. 149). After this, however, Lyford and Oldham continue to practice one deception after another until God intervenes:

> But it so pleased God that the bark that carried him [Oldham] and many other passengers was in that danger as they despaired of life; so as many of them, as they fell to prayer, so also did they begin to examine their consciences and confess such sins as did most burthen them. And Mr. Oldham did make a free and large confession of the wrongs and hurt he had done to the people and church here, in many particulars, that as he had sought their ruin, so God had now met with him and might destroy him. (p. 165)

Oldham's life is spared, he confesses his sins, he makes peace with the people. This is his last act:

> At length, going a trading in a small vessel among the Indians, and being weakly manned, upon some quarrel they knocked him in the head with a hatchet so as he fell down dead and never spake word more. (p. 166)

There is little doubt that his death is directly the result of the just hand of God.

"I am now come to Mr. Lyford," says Bradford prophetically. "But first behold the hand of God concerning him, wherein that of the Psalmist is verified: Psalm vii.15: 'He hath made a pit and digged it, and is fallen into the pit he made'" (p. 166). Lyford is doomed. His past is quickly unveiled, particularly his adultery. After he leaves his friends at Naumkeag (Salem), he goes to Virginia "where he shortly after died; and so I leave him to the Lord" (p. 169).

The parallel drawn between Lyford and Ishmael in sentence 5, paragraph 1, signals that biblical analogy remains a structural principle. Ishmael is the type; Lyford is the antitype. As God intervened to shield Abraham, Sarah, and Isaac from the ill feelings and dissemblings of Hagar and Ishmael, He now intervenes to protect His people of Plymouth from the gross deceptions and evil practices of Lyford and Oldham.

As usual, the imagery also invites one to draw an analogy between Christ's passion and the Pilgrims' sufferings. Lyford betrays them many times. The sinking imagery that evolves from the coupling "bowed and cringed" (sentence 3, paragraph 1) which refers to Lyford, ironically enough, is transferred implicitly to the Pilgrims. As a result of Lyford's actions, many of them are lowered in the eyes of such upright men as Bradford and, most significantly, in the eyes of God. But from all of this, God works some good. As a direct result of the Lyford affair, some Pilgrims are reborn and rise to a closer relationship with God through membership in His church:

> The winter was passed over in their ordinary affairs, without any special matter worth noting; saving that many who before stood something off from the church, now seeing Lyford's unrighteous dealing and malignity against the church, now tendered themselves to the church and were joined to the same; professing that it was not out of the dislike of anything that they had stood off so long,

103

but a desire to fit themselves better for such a state, and they saw now the Lord called for their help.

And so these troubles produced a quite contrary effect, in sundry here, than these adversaries hoped for. Which was looked at as a great work of God, to draw on men by unlikely means, and that in reason which might rather have set them further off. (pp. 163-164)

Without a doubt, the movement from the visible to the invisible and back to the visible world is the most pertinent structural principle of the whole episode. The first two and a half sentences of paragraph 1 reveal all too briefly a visible world. But this is to be expected when dealing with the likes of Lyford, a minister who thrives on deception. The Pilgrims see Lyford come ashore. After that, his bowing and cringing, his willingness to kiss "their hands if they would have suffered him," his weeping and shedding of tears, his blessing "God that had brought him to see their faces," his "admiring the things they had done in their wants," his acting "as if he had been made all of love and the humblest person in the world"-- all of these complexly simultaneous acts create an incredible distortion of vision until God intervenes near the end of the episode.

In sentence 3, paragraph 2, Bradford says:

He made a large confession of his faith, and an acknowledgment of his former disorderly walking and his being entangled with many corruptions, which had been a burthen to his conscience, and blessed God for this opportunity of freedom and liberty to enjoy the ordinances of God in purity among His People; with many more such like expressions.

It is these "expressions" that appear to deceive momentarily even such a godly person as Bradford, supposedly the most perceptive character in the history: "Now whether this was in hypocrisy, or

104

out of some sudden pang of conviction, which I
rather think, God only knows" (p. 149). It is also
"such like expressions" that are repeated over and
over again, maintaining the state of invisibility.

Almost immediately following this extravagant
confession, Lyford and Oldham conspire to send some
letters to England, defaming Bradford and the
planters; "yet outwardly they still set a fair face
of things" (p. 149). When their "dissembling" is
discovered, they deny everything vehemently at
first, but later confess: "Lyford acknowledged his
censure was far less than he deserved. Afterward,
he confessed his sin publicly in the church with
tears more largely than before" (p. 157).

It is this inability of the planters to
find the private Lyford in the public that dis-
torts their vision the most. Surprisingly, after
Lyford's second confession, the planters

> began again to conceive good thoughts of
> him upon this his repentance, and admitted
> him to teach amongst them as before; and
> Samuel Fuller (a deacon amongst them) and
> some other tenderhearted men amongst them,
> were so taken with his signs of sorrow and
> repentance, as they professed they would fall
> upon their knees to have his censure released.
> (p. 158)

Obviously, Bradford is no longer deceived, but for
the majority of the planters, things remain primarily invisible.

Lyford makes one last bold attempt to sustain
the state of invisibility: he writes another
letter to the adventurers in England, this time
justifying "all his former writings." Yet it is a
desperate and futile act. Acting against Lyford
and for the Pilgrims, God intercedes and restores
visibility. The Pilgrims, "now seeing Lyford's
unrighteous dealing and malignity against the
church, now tendered themselves to the church and
were joined to the same" (p. 163). With God's
help, more of Lyford's deceptions are exposed:

In the meantime, God in His providence had detected Lyford's evil carriage in Ireland to some friends amongst the company, who made it known to Mr. Winslow and directed him to two godly and grave witnesses who would testify the same, if called there unto, upon their oath. (p. 168)

The private Lyford is now clearly visible. He is nothing more than a crafty confidence man who hoped to use the ministry to conceal his lust and schemes. Too formidable an opponent for the Pilgrims, what else can they do but "leave him to the Lord"?

Collocation confirms much of what has been said above. Many of the nouns and verbs in the whole Lyford episode collocate easily around the nodal items discussed previously. Beginning with the reference to "came ashore" in sentence 3, paragraph 1, many words and phrases throughout the episode suggest that its chief concern is with a voyage, e.g., "ship," "England," "paradise," "Holland," "master of the ship," "a league or two at sea," "came hither"--the list is almost endless. Specifically, it is a voyage toward visibility, understanding, perception, and God. The Pilgrims' sea of troubles is Lyford and Oldham. Though they do not realize it, Lyford and Oldham are also on a voyage toward God. Their sea of troubles is their own inability to control the vast discrepancies between their private and public selves.

Most words are collocates of verbs of seeing. There is ample evidence for this assertion in the two initial paragraphs to the Lyford episode. Paragraph 1 contains such words and phrases as "seen," "to see their faces," "his after carriages," "dissembling Ishmael," and "met them." Paragraph 2 contains such phrases as "such like expressions." From this point, there are many words and phrases related to sight: "to open his mind," "saw," "seemed," "discovered," "letters," "concealed," "see," "privately," "appear," "seek," "deceived," "sent copies of them," "confessed in open court,"

106

"to be examined," "showing," "proof," "witness,"
"evidence," "dissemblings," "eye," "publicly,"
"secretly," "face," "expressions," "public confession," "tears," "seeing," "looked at," "behold
the hand of God," "opens his own to all the world,"
"dark and secret mutterings," and "evidence so
plain" (pp. 149-169).

Unquestionably in an episode of this length
from a writer as conscious of style as Bradford is,
assonance contributes to unity and coherence (for
example, one sees this briefly in the first two
Lyford paragraphs: can, man, hands, etc.). But
the sound device that captures one's attention is
the words with initial /s/ sounds. If there is one
word which can describe the acts of a minister who
perverts the duties and responsibilities of his
office, that word is "sin." All words which begin
with an /s/ sound revolve around "sin," and there
are many of them. Paragraph 1 for instance,
contains "sent," "saluted," "seldom," "seen," "so,"
"suffered," "see," and "saying." The remainder of
the episode includes such words as "slander,"
"subversion," "sealed," "sly," "stiff," "scurrilous," "scarce," "censure," "struck," "silent,"
"special," "sell," "stolen," "sought," "strange,"
and "spoiled" (pp. 149-155). Although there are
words which begin with an /s/ sound and are not as
negative as many of these, the negative ones seem
to outweigh the positive. Add to this list the
many negative words that have the /s/ sound either
near the middle or at the final position (e.g.,
hypocrisy, perverse, false, accusations, adversary,
concealed, quarrels, refused, rascal, furious,
traitors, rebels, resisted, insolent, forsake,
furiously, intercepted, discontent, deceived,
conspiracy, treacherously, mischief, disgraceful,
audacious, mutinous, etc.) and the image can be
none other than that of a serpent, a demon.

Two lengthy antithetic relationships which
grow out of Lyford's inconstancy also provide unity
and coherence. The first one occurs when Lyford
comes ashore with undue reverence and humility,
bowing, crying, admiring, blessing, making a "large

confession of his faith," and asking forgiveness for the wrongs he inflicted against the Pilgrims. "But," remarks Bradford, "this lasted not long, for both Oldham and he grew very perverse, and showed a spirit of great malignancy, drawing many into faction as they could" (p. 149). The church which he had earlier expressed a desire to "join himself a member to," he now speaks profanely against in "private meetings and whisperings."

The second antithetic relationship concerns the secret letters that Lyford writes to the adventurers, accusing Bradford and his people of much wrongdoing. After Bradford discovers the letters, Lyford denies everything: he "burst out in tears, and confessed he 'feared he was a reprobate, his sins were so great that he doubted God would pardon them, he was unsavory salt,' etc" (p. 157). This emotional confession deceives many people, including deacon Samuel Fuller. "But," says Bradford,

> that which made them all stand amazed in the end, and may do all others that shall come to hear the same (for a rarer precedent can scarce be shown) was, that after a month or two, notwithstanding all his former confessions, convictions, and public acknowledgments, both in the face of the church and the whole company, with so many tears and sad censures of himself before God and men, he should go again to justify what he had done. (p. 158)

For he writes a second letter to the adventurers.

That the repetition of words and the use of synonyms are devices of unity and coherence has already been demonstrated in the discussion of the collocation of verbs of seeing. The sight words in paragraphs 1 and 2 such as "seen," "see," "faces," "tears," "dissembling," "confessions," and "expressions" are repeated over and over, as well as their numerous synonyms and collocates. These words never permit one to forget that Lyford's most prominent characteristic is deception.

The fourth set of paragraphs occurs in chapter 19 and recounts the dissemblings of another Lyford-like character, Thomas Morton. Like Lyford's, Morton's conduct and schemes move Bradford ("O, the horribleness of his villainy!") to comment at length before anything like a resolution is reached. Consequently, one finds it necessary again to discuss the paragraphs in context of the complete episode so that the whole of all structural patterns can be fully appreciated. The paragraphs are somewhat long, but I feel it is necessary to record them in full in order to capture the flavor of this particular moment in the history:

> About some three or four years before this time, there came over one Captain Wollaston (a man of pretty parts) and with him three or four more of some eminency, who brought with them a great many servants, with provisions and other implements for to begin a plantation. And pitched themselves in a place within Massachusetts which they called after their Captain's name, Mount Wollaston. Amongst them was one Mr. Morton, who it should seem had some small adventure of his own or other men's amongst them, but had little respect amongst them, and was slighted by the meanest servants. Having continued there some time, and not finding things to answer their expectations nor profit to arise as they looked for, Captain Wollaston takes a great part of the servants and transports them to Virginia, where he puts them off at good rates, selling their time to other men; and writes back to one Mr. Rasdall (one of his chief partners and accounted their merchant) to bring another part of them to Virginia likewise, intending to put them off there as he had done the rest. And he, with the consent of the said Rasdall, appointed one Fitcher to be his Lieutenant and govern the remains of the Plantation till he or Rasdall returned to

take further order thereabout. But this
Morton abovesaid, having more craft than
honesty (who had been a kind of pettifogger of
Furnival's Inn) in the others' absence watches
an opportunity (commons being but hard amongst
them) and got some strong drink and other
junkets and made them a feast; and after they
were merry, he began to tell them he would
give them good counsel. "You see," saith he,
"that many of your fellows are carried to
Virginia, and if you stay till this Rasdall
return, you will also be carried away and sold
for slaves with the rest. Therefore I would
advise you to thrust out this Lieutenant
Fitcher, and I, having a part in the Plantation, will receive you as my partners and
consociates; so may you be free from service,
and we will converse, plant, trade, and live
together as equals and support and protect one
another," or to like effect. This counsel was
easily received, so they took opportunity and
thrust Lieutenant Fitcher out o' doors, and
would suffer him to come no more amongst them,
but forced him to seek bread to eat and other
relief from his neighbours till he could get
passage to England.

After this they fell to great licentious-
ness and led a dissolute life, pouring out
themselves into all profaneness. And Morton
became Lord of Misrule, and maintained (as
it were) a School of Atheism. And after they
had got some goods into their hands, and much
by trading with the Indians, they spent it
as vainly in quaffing and drinking, both wine
and strong waters in great excess (and, as
some reports) £10 worth in a morning. They
also set up a maypole, drinking and dancing
about it many days together, inviting the
Indian women for their consorts, dancing and
frisking together like so many fairies, or
furies, rather; and worse practices. As
if they had anew revived and celebrated
the feasts of the Roman goddess Flora, or the
beastly practices of the mad Bacchanalians.

110

Morton likewise, to show his poetry composed
sundry rhymes and verses, some tending to
lasciviousness, and others to the detraction
and scandal of some persons, which he affixed
to this idle or idol maypole. They changed
also the name of their place, and instead of
calling it Mount Wollaston they called it
Merry-mount, as if this jollity would have
lasted ever. But this continued not long, for
after Morton was sent for England (as follows
to be declared) shortly after came over that
worthy gentlemen Mr. John Endecott, who
brought over a patent under the broad seal for
the government of the Massachusetts. Who,
visiting those parts, caused that maypole to
be cut down and rebuked them for their profaneness and admonished them to look there
should be better walking. So they or other
now changed the name of their place again and
called it Mount Dagon. (pp. 205-206)

An examination of the stress groups of paragraph 2 indicates that binary stress groups remain a major characteristic of Bradford's rhythm--
a rhythm which is tied closely to the couplings.
The stress groups for sentence 1 are 2, 3, 3, 3,
and 2:

After this / they fell to great licentious-
ness / and led a dissolute life, / pouring out
themselves / into all profaneness.

4, 2, and 2 is the pattern of stress groups in
sentence 2:

And Morton became Lord of Misrule, / and
maintained (as it were) / a School of Atheism.

Sentence 3 divides into stress groups of 4, 2, 1,
2, 2, 2, 2, 2, and 2:

111

And after they had got some goods into their
hands, / and got much by trading / with the
Indians, / they spent it vainly / in quaffing
and drinking, / both wine and strong waters
/ in great excess / (and, as some reported) /
£10 worth in a morning.

Regardless of the number of stresses in a foot,
the rhythm that one hears is that which derives
from and is controlled by such piling up of couplings as "quaffing and drinking, both wine and
strong waters." Though there may be stress
groups of 3, 4, 5, or 6 stresses, the couplings
return the rhythm to two stress groups, just as
surely as almost every paragraph in the history
returns to the "Spirit of God and His grace." The
stress groups of sentence 4 are 3, 3, 3, 4, 3, 2,
2, and 2:

They also set up a maypole, / drinking and
dancing about it / many days together, /
inviting the Indian women for their consorts,
/ dancing and frisking together / like so many
fairies, / or furies, rather; / and worse
practices.

The stress groups of sentence 5 are 4, 4, and 4:

As if they had anew revived and celebrated
/ the feasts of the Roman goddess Flora, / or
the beastly practices of the mad Bacchanalians.

Stress groups expand, creating cadences and matching Bradford's increasing distaste for Morton.
The pattern of the stress groups in sentence 6 is
2, 2, 4, 2, 4, 2, and 3:

> Morton likewise, / to show his poetry ′ com-
> posed sundry rhymes and verses, / some
> tending to lasciviousness, / and others to the
> detraction and scandal of some persons, /
> which he affixed ′ to this idle or idol
> maypole.

2, 2, 4, 2, 2, and 2 are the stress groups for
sentence 7:

> They changed also ′ the name of their place, /
> and instead of calling it Mount Wollaston /
> they call it Merry-mount, / as if this jollity
> ′ would have lasted ever.

Sentence 8 divides into stress groups of 3, 4, 2,
2, 3, 2, 2, 2, and 2:

> But this continued not long, / for after
> Morton was sent for England / (as follows to
> be declared) / shortly after ′ came over that
> worthy gentleman ′ Mr. John Endecott, / who
> brought over a patent ′ under the broad seal
> ′ for the government of the Massachusetts.

Sentence 9 divides into stress groups of 1, 2, 2,
2, 3, and 5:

> Who, / visiting those parts, / caused that
> maypole / to be cut down / and rebuked them
> for their profaneness / and admonished them to
> look there should be better walking.

And the stress groups of sentence 10 are 2, 4, and 3:

> So they or others / now changed the name
> of their place again / and called it Mount
> Dagon.

Though the first paragraph does not contain any
couplings, the second contains more couplings than
any paragraph examined thus far. They are "quaffing and drinking," "wine and strong waters,"
"drinking and dancing," "dancng and frisking,"
"fairies, or furies," "revived and celebrated,"
"rhymes and verses," "detraction and scandal," and
"idle or idol." Indeed, the couplings beat out the
time for Morton's dances. The fact that "idle" and
"idol" are phonetically identical / / seems to
confirm a point made earlier that the near similarity of the couplings denies choice or alternatives. The couplings give only the appearance of
choice, just as the Pilgrims appear to have many
allternatives when they only have one.

     The notion of alternatives, therefore, remains
of major importance to Bradford. Although it
concerns a different character, the argument is
essentially the same as it was in the first paragraph of the history. But if the reader or the
"children of these fathers" is to see and know the
ways of God, the argument must be redundant.
Seeing is everything. "God," says Bradford late in
the history, "it seems, would have all men to
behold and observe all such mercies and works of
His providence as these are towards His people,
that they in like cases might be encouraged to
depend upon God in their trials, and also to bless

His name when they see His goodness towards others"
(p. 329).

Practically every sentence in these paragraphs
begins either with an additive connective or with
an adversative one, not to mention the many intrasentence ones, especially the alternative ones.
These connectives give the argument persuasiveness,
logic, clarity, and form.   While they detest him
tremendously, the Pilgrims can do little or nothing
with Morton.   They turn first to John Endecott,
"who, visiting these parts, caused the maypole to
be cut down and rebuked them for their profaneness
and admonished them to look there should be better
walking."   This does little good; Morton's people
simply change the name of their place to Mount
Dagon.

Maintaining "this riotous prodigality and
profuse excess," Morton starts trading "pieces,
powder and shot to the Indians," to the great
hazard of the Dutch and English.   Bradford feels
that many people have become innocent victims as a
direct result of Morton's actions.

Perceiving that Morton becomes daily "more
haughty and insolent," some people of Massachusetts
ask Bradford to send Captain Standish and others to
take Morton by force.   More as a result of their
own drunkeness than anything else, Morton and his
people are finally taken captive.   Morton is sent
to the Council of New England for punishment, but
nothing happens to him.   He goes next to England
and

> yet nothing was done to him, not so much as
> rebuked, for aught was heard, but returned the
> next year.   Some of the worst of the company
> were dispersed and some of the more modest
> kept the house till he should be heard from.
> But I have been too long about so unworthy a
> person, and bad a cause.   (p. 210)

Like Lyford, Morton proves too formidable a foe.
All Bradford can do is drop him from the narrative

and leave him to the Lord. Quoting from Proverbs later in the history, he writes: "'the memorial of the just shall be blessed, when the name of the wicked shall rot'" and adds parenthetically: "with their marble monuments" (p. 325).

The references to biblical events and the imagery suggest that typology or biblical analogy is still a structural pattern. Morton's tempting of the people of Mount Wollaston to betray Lieutenant Fitcher recalls Satan's tempting of Eve and the expulsion of Adam and Eve from the Garden. Getting them "some strong drink and other junkets," preparing "them a feast," and making them "merry," Morton speaks to the people in words reminiscent of Satan's: "I . . . will receive you as my partners and consociates; so may you be free from service, and we will converse, plant, trade, and live together as equals and support and protect one another" (emphasis mine). Equality is what Satan promises Eve and is cursed for his efforts; Morton, the cause of Fitcher's expulsion, is expelled himself. As such, he seems to embody characteristics of both Satan and Eve.

The overriding image is one of suffering, and there is little doubt that Bradford places the Pilgrims' sufferings in the context of Christ's. Because of Morton's betrayal, because of his trading of guns and powder with the Indians, the Pilgrims encounter severe hardships: "It was terror unto them who lived stragglingly and were of no strength in any place" (p. 208). Once the Indians' appetite is stimulated by guns, there is nothing they will not do to get more of them. Many Dutch and English "have been lately slain by those Indians thus furnished" (p. 208). Interestingly enough, God does not intervene immediately this time. This is probably because uncertainty is steadily creeping into the history--uncertainty about the Pilgrims' role as God's chosen people. But if Bradford is certain of anything, he is positive that it is God who upholds and sustains. While the straggling plantations have to rely on such men as Bradford and Standish for immediate help, the implication at the end of the episode is that the whole issue has been left to God, who will eventually give Morton the punishment he deserves and restore things to a state of normalcy. It is only when God acts on men, whether they are good or bad, that a sense of stability and permanence is achieved. It is a rare occurrence in the history when man succeeds of his own power. Man, it seems Bradford would have one conclude, is totally helpless without God's assistance.

Understanding Morton is mainly a problem of perception. Consequently, the movement from the visible to the invisible and back to the visible world becomes essential to the structure and meaning of the whole Morton affair. The first part of paragraph 1 introduces the visible world. Captain Wollaston, a man of some wealth, attempts to establish a plantation within the Massachusetts Bay Colony. Not finding the profit he desires, Wollaston takes a large part of his servants and moves to Virginia, "where he puts them off at good rates, selling their time to other men." He later instructs Mr. Rasdall to bring the remainder of the servants and appoints Fitcher his (Wollaston's) Lieutenant until he or Rasdall can return to Mount Wollaston.

With Morton's introduction however, things shift quickly into invisibility. Morton, who is "slighted by the meanest servants," possesses "more craft than honesty"; he is a "pettifogger" who "in the others' absence watches an opportunity" to practice deception. He blinds the people of Mount Wollaston with "drink and other junkets." The feast which he organizes provides additional concealment of his schemes, divorcing the people further and further from reality. The feast is a mad and frenzied scene, with Bradford piling up coupling after coupling in order to penetrate Morton's mask. Bradford is not sure whether the people are fairies or furies, whether they are celebrating the "feasts of the Roman goddess Flora, or the beastly practices of the mad Bacchanalians."

Bringing a new patent, "that worthy gentleman Mr. John Endecott" comes to the colony, orders the maypole's destruction, reprimands the people for their profaneness, and admonishes them "to look there should be better walking" (emphasis mine). These acts restore visibility momentarily. The fact that the people change the name of their settlement from Merry-mount to Mount Dagon revives the state of invisibility. Dagon, the chief god of the ancient Philistines and later of the Phoenicians, is a fitting example of invisibility and complexity: the form that he takes is that of half-man and half-fish. Morton maintains "this riotous prodigality and profuse excess" by selling guns to the Indians. Using these guns to harass the Dutch and the English, particularly the outlying settlements, the Indians become extensions of the invisible state intitiated by Morton.

Bradford, Standish, and others are only able to restore things to a partially visible state. They take Morton captive and disperse some of his people. As in the case of Lyford, only God can restore total visibility, and the implication is that He eventually will.

The use of the fowl metaphor, "if this nest was not broken" (p. 208), adds a new structural pattern. The metaphor begins with the reference to Morton's teaching the Indians "what shot to use for fowl and what for deer" (p. 206). He employs the Indians to "hunt fowl for him," since they are more adept at hunting than any of the English. "So as the Indians are full of pieces all over," laments Bradford, "both fowling pieces, muskets, pistols, etc. They have also their moulds to make shot of all sorts, as musket bullets, pistol bullets, swan and goose shot, and of smaller sorts" (p. 207). All the references to fowls, hunting of fowls, fowling pieces, swans and geese shot culminate in "all the scum of the country or any discontents would flock to him from all places, if this nest was not broken" (p. 208). This very appropriate image of the dispersal of a flock of birds dominates the rest of the Morton passages.

118

Most of the nouns and verbs are collocates of the nodal items voyage, sea of troubles, and Lord. Some of the words and phrases in paragraph 1 that are collocates of voyage are "came over," "provisions," "other implements," "to begin a plantation," "adventure," "profit," "transports," "Virginia," "merchant," "to bring another part of them," "carried," "carried away," "partners and consociates," "together," "support," "bread to eat," and "passage." Some of those in paragraph 2 are "sent for England," "came over," "visiting those parts," and "better walking."

While there is a variety of voyagers and while all do not possess a clear sense of purpose, the destination is essentially the same. Wollaston and Rasdall are on a voyage toward God, but it is a journey toward His punishment. Their sea of troubles includes a great deal, but of primary significance is avarice, the obsession to make things "answer their expectations," the ardent desire for "profit." They have no real sense of purpose or direction. Unlike the Pilgrims, who sometimes experience a temporary loss of direction (as, for example, in the foregrounded and trip to Holland passages), they seem permanently blind and lost. It is as if they create myths for the deception of others, yet believe in them themselves. The same can be said of Thomas Morton.

Bradford, other Pilgrims, and the reader (the children of these fathers) are on a voyage too. Morton, Wollaston, and Rasdall represent one more obstacle or test (sea of troubles) that must be overcome. Although the Pilgrims have a clear sense of mission, they are not without fault. After all, it is the desire for profit that causes some of them to leave Plymouth in 1632, weakening the church and destroying the sense of community.

Many of the verbs are collocates of verbs of seeing. In paragraph 1, there are such words as "seem," "to arise," "looked," "absence," "watches," "see," and "to seek." In paragraph 2, there are "to show" and "look." Since the idea of a feast

dominates this scene, there are numerous words that
are collocates of verbs of tasting, e.g., "to eat"
and "drinking."

The alliterative patterns in paragraph 2 give
unity and meaning to the whole episode. All
significant alliterative patterns in this episode are beautifully compressed into paragraph 2;
all have their origin there. Initial /d/ sounds
are quite prominent: "dissolute," "drinking,"
"drinking and dancing," "days," "dancing," "detraction," "declared," "down," "Dagon." (The
movement from "dissolute" to "Dagon" captures the
essence of Morton and his followers.) Key words in
other paragraphs begin with the same sound:
"defense," "daily," "danger," "Dutch," "digression," "discontents," "displeasure," and "dis-
persed" (pp. 206-210).

Many words with initial /p/ sounds occur in
paragraph 2: "pour" "profaneness," "practices,"
"practices," "poetry," "persons," "place," "patent," "parts," "profaneness," and "place." Words
in other paragraphs with the same initial sound are
"pretty parts," "provisions," "plantation," "profit," "partners," "pettifogger," "protect," and
"passage" in paragraph 1; "prodigality and profuse,"
"powder," "pieces," "proportion," "practice," and
"price" in paragraph 3; "parts," "pieces," "pistols," "pistol," "powder," "pound," "places,"
"pound," and "powder" in paragraph 4; "provided,"
"princes and parliaments," "present," "punishment,"
and "parts" in paragraph 5; "pieces," "place,"
"places," and "prevented" in paragraph 6; "plantations," "Plymouth," "prevent," "Piscataqua," and
"places" in paragraph 7; "proclamation," "pen-
ality," "persisted," and "prepare" in paragraph 8;
"proceed," "Plymouth," "powder," and "point" in
paragraph 9.

Significant initial /m/ sound words in paragraph 2 are "Morton," "Misrule," "maintained,"
"much," "morning," "maypole," "many," "many,"
"mad," "Morton," "maypole," "Morton," "Mount"
(Wollaston), "Merry-mont," "Morton," "Massa-

chusetts," "maypole," and "Mount" (Dagon). Other words which begin with an /m/ sound (many of which are repeated like those above) are "man," "many," "Morton," "meanest," "merchant," "merry," "mischief," "musket," and "murder."

Important initial /f/ sounds in paragraph 2 are "fell," "frisking," "fairies," "furies," "feasts," and "Flora." Some of the words with similar initial sounds in other paragraphs are "finding," "Fitcher," "free," "feast," "French," "fisherman," "fowl," "fitted and furnished," "friends," "flock," and "force"; many of these recur again and again.

The patterns for words with similar vowel sounds in the stressed syllable are set in paragraph 2. For example, there are words with the /ɔr/ sound: "pouring," "Morton," "Lord" (of Misrule), "morning," "consorts," "Flora," "for," and "shortly." Some words in other passages with a similar vowel sound are "Morton," "nor," "order," "consortship," "sorts," "ordinarily," "war," "consort," "score," and "short."

With "feast" and "beast" being the leading examples in paragraph 2, a few additional words have the /i/ vowel sound: "he," "seal," and "be." There are numerous words in other paragraphs with the same vowel sound: "three," "seem," "feast," "sea," "free," "eat," "relief," "piece," etc. There are also many words with the /ɛ/ vowel sound such as in "excess" and "nest."

Quite a few words in paragraph 2 have the /e/ vowel sound, many of which are repeated: "they," "great," "profaneness," "became," "maintained," "Atheism," "vainly," "maypole," "days," "changed," "name," and "place." Similar vowel sounds occur abundantly throughout, e.g., "rates," "gain," "same," "occasion," "base," "danger," "slain," and "traitors."

The repetition of the "ing" suffix is a common device of unity and coherence in Bradford's history; it is essentially a standard feature of his style. Yet there are few places in the history where this characteristic occurs so profusely as in paragraph 2: "Pouring," "trading," "quaffing and drinking," "drinking and dancing," "inviting," "dancing and frisking," "tending," "calling," "visiting," and "walking." Other passages make use of the same device: "finding," "intending," "being," "having," "thinking," "knowing," "accounting," "prevailing," "fowling," and "meeting."

Although Bradford frequently repeats parallel and balanced infinitive phrases, prepositional phrases, relative clauses, and noun phrase complements, his favorite device of unity and coherence is antithesis. All of the passages about Morton work in terms of antithetic relations, with "but" or "so" signaling the beginning of the contrast. The first half of paragraph 1, for instance, recounts Captain Wollaston's flight to Virginia after not finding any profit in the Massachusetts colony. Captain Wollaston makes plans with Fitcher to govern in his (Wollaston's) absence. "But," says Bradford, "this Morton abovesaid, having more craft than honesty (who had been a kind of pettifogger of Furnival's Inn) in the others' absence watches an opportunity . . . and got some strong drink and other junkets and made them a feast." Morton creates the exact opposite of the government or perhaps order that Wollaston hopes to leave behind.

The first part of paragraph 2 relates a mad and wild event: people are trading, spending, drinking, inviting, and frisking. Morton is dubbed Lord of Misrule, a very dubious honor. "But," remarks Bradford, "this continued not long." Endecott has the maypole destroyed and admonishes the people to amend their ways. But even this state of order is extremely short-lived. As the last sentence tells, the people simply change the name of their place and call it Mount Dagon.

Events in Bradford's Of Plymouth Plantation suggest a world of contrasts. Nowhere in the history is the difficulty of recording the events of such a world presented more clearly than in the Morton episode. The calm and objective tone of the preface momentarily vanishes when Bradford speaks of Morton; yielding to Morton's contrasting world, the tone splits into extremes: subjectivity and objectivity. Deeply moved by the actions of Morton and his followers, Bradford cries out, "O, the horribleness of this villainy!" He calls them "gain-thirsty murderers," and asks that "princes and parliaments" provide some "exemplary punishment." "But," says Bradford as he realizes his momentary engulfment by Morton's world, "I have forgot myself and have been too long in this digression; but now to return" to the Morton story, but most importantly, to his former objective tone, which is the proper one for a historian interested in "the simple truth in all things."

Antithesis dominates the remainder of the episode. The outlying settlements write Morton "in a friendly and neighbourly way to admonish him to forbear those courses, and sent a messenger with their letters to bring his answer" (p.209). "But he was so high as he scorned all advice, and asked who had to do with him, he had and would trade pieces with the Indians, in despite of all, with many other scurrilous terms full of disdain" (p. 209). They send him a second letter, arguing that his actions are against their common safety and the King's proclamation, "but insolently he persisted and said the King was dead and his displeasure with him, and many the like things" (p. 209). They conclude that physical coercion is the only way to subdue him, "but they found him to stand stiffly in his defense, having made fast his doors, armed his consorts, set divers dishes of powder and bullets ready on the table" (p. 209).

More than any other words, the repetition of "see," "Morton," "maypole," and "feast" and the use of their various synonyms and collocates give unity and coherence to the Morton passages. "See" occurs in all of its principal parts. It also has numerous collocates, e.g., "looked for," "to seek,"

"to show," "to look," and "quicksighted." The name
"Morton" is repeated over and over again, creating
a hammering effect; all pejorative words can easily
be considered either synonyms or collocates of it,
and there are many of them, e.g., "Misrule,"
"School of Atheism," "wicked man," "wicked and
debased," "riotous prodigality and profuse excess"
--the list is almost infinite. As in a litany
where the ritualistic repetition of an evil supposedly expels it, the word "maypole" is hammered
again and again, much in the same fashion as
Morton's name. Many references are made to "feast"
and food. In the two opening paragraphs, "feasts"
occurs twice, with each reference strategically
placed in separate paragraphs. In the second
paragraph, there is also a reference to "bread to
eat." As the episode progresses, "feasts" is
supplanted by "fowl," "fowling pieces," and finally
by "these gain-thirsty murderers." Of all words
and phrases which are repeated, the many references
to food contribute most to unity and coherence.
Interestingly enough, Bradford even conceives of
this "debased crew" in terms of food. They are a
"flock" of birds whose "nest" must be broken.

Although his argument is quite persuasive,
Bradford's opinion of Morton should not necessarily
be taken as fact, especially his claim that Morton
initiates the sale of guns and ammunition to the
Indians. Obsessed with the desire to overthrow
Morton's plantation, Bradford may well have been
tempted to use any means to rid Plymouth of Morton.
Perhaps Bradford, as Minor W. Major argues, is more
disturbed by the relations which some of Morton's
men have with the Indian women than by the more
noted offense. Since there is no law in England
forbidding sexual relations with Indian women,
there is no chance that Morton will be punished on
such a charge. Thus, Bradford concocts a charge
that is in clear violation of the proclamation
against the sale of arms. Three facts convince
Major that Bradford's accusation against Morton is
suspect. First, Bradford's verse "Account of New
England" indicates that he has no real evidence
that anyone in his vicinity has sold guns to the

Indians. Second, the official records of Morton's trial and deportation say nothing about illegal arms trade, either in Plymouth or elsewhere. Third, the fact that no action is taken in England against Morton suggests that Bradford is unable to produce any concrete evidence of illegal activity.[2]

The next paragraph is in chapter 33 and is a biography of William Brewster:

I am to begin this year with that which was a matter of great sadness and mourning unto them all. About the 18th of April died their Reverend Elder and my dear and loving friend Mr. William Brewster, a man that had done and suffered much for the Lord Jesus and the gospel's sake, and had borne his part in weal and woe with this poor persecuted church above 36 years in England, Holland and in this wilderness, and done the Lord and them faithful service in his place and calling. And notwithstanding the many troubles and sorrows he passed through, the Lord upheld him to a great age. He was near fourscore years of age (if not all out) when he died. He had this blessing added by the Lord to all the rest; to die in his bed, in peace, amongst the midst of his friends, who mourned and wept over him, and he again recomforted them whilst he could. His sickness was not long, and till the last day thereof he did not wholly keep his bed. His speech continued till somewhat more than half a day, and then failed him, and about nine or ten a clock that evening he died without any pangs at all. A few hours before, he drew his breath short, and some few minutes before his last, he drew his breath long as a man fallen into a sound sleep without any pangs or gaspings, and so sweetly departed this life unto a better. (p. 324)

The stress groups for sentence 1 are 3, 5, and 2:

        I am to begin this year / with that which was
        a matter of great sadness and mourning / unto
        them all.

The stress patterns for sentence 2 are 2, 2, 3, 2,
6, 2, 2, 2, 7, 2, 3, 2, and 2:
        About the 18th of April / died their Reverend
        Elder / and my dear and loving friend / Mr.
        William Brewster, / a man that had done and
        suffered much for the Lord Jesus / and the
        gospel's sake, / and had borne his part / in
        weal and woe / with this poor persecuted
        church above 36 years in England, Holland
        / and in this wilderness, / and done the Lord
        and them / faithful service / in his place and
        calling.

The alliterative seven-stress cadence in the ninth
foot recalls a similar one in the first foregrounded passage: "this poor people's present
condition." 4, 2, 2, and 2 is the pattern of the
stress groups in sentence 3:
        And notwithstanding the many troubles and
        sorrows / he passed through, / the Lord upheld
        him / to a great age.

The stress groups of sentence 4 are 4, 2, and 1:
        He was near fourscore years of age / (if not
        all out) / when he died.

126

The stress groups seem directly related to time.
They increase in number in the first foot, emphasizing Brewster's long eighty-year life span.
Since death represents an abrupt end to Brewster's
longevity, the stress groups decrease in number as
the sentence approaches the word "died." This
sentence demonstrates well how rhythm is sometimes
tied to meaning.   Sentence 5 divides into stress
groups of 2, 3, 2, 1, 3, 3, 4, and 2:

He had this blessing , added by the Lord to

all the rest; / to die in his bed, / in peace,

/ amongst the midst of his friends, / who

mourned and wept over him , and ministered

what help and comfort they could / unto

him.

This is a very quiet and reflective moment in
the history.   The one stress that falls on "in
peace" does much toward enhancing such a mood. 2,
3, and 4 is the pattern of the stress groups in
sentence 6:

His sickness was not long, / and till the last

day thereof , he did not wholly keep his

bed.

The stress groups grow in number as the sentence
grows toward its major concern: "he did not wholly
keep his bed"; the rhythm matches the climactic
order of the sentence perfectly.

    The stress groups of sentence 7 are 5, 2, 5,
and 4:

His speech continued till somewhat more than

half a day, / and then failed him, / and about

nine or ten a clock that evening ; he died
without any pangs at all.

Again, rhythm and climactic order are closely
allied. The last sentence falls into stress groups
of 2, 2, 4, 9, 3, and 2:

A few hours before, / he drew his breath

short, / and some few minutes before his last,

/ he drew his breath long as a man fallen into

a sound sleep without any pangs or gaspings, /

and so sweetly departed this life ; unto a

better.

The lengthy nine-stress group complements the image
of breathing long. As Brewster departs quietly
toward a better life, the final binary stress group
provides a quiet reminder of the dominant role
binary stresses play in the history. Although the
argument that Bradford's rhythm is mainly one of
binary stress groups (which emerge from the strik-
ing number of couplings) may be somewhat contro-
versial, there should be little or no controversy
in the assertion that the iamb and anapest occur
more than any other foot. After several paragraphs into the history, one anticipates the iamb
and anapest much as he does the couplings. Like
the couplings, they can easily be considered a
pertinent structural pattern on the basis of their
repetition.

As in the second paragraph about Morton, the
couplings in this paragraph are numerous. With the
exception of sentences 4, 6, and 7, every sentence
contains at least one coupling. There is "sadness
and mourning" in sentence 1; "dear and loving,"
"done and suffered," "weal and woe," and "place and
calling" in sentence 2; "troubles and sorrows" in
sentence 3; "mourned and wept," and "help and

comfort" in sentence 5; and "pangs or gaspings" in
sentence 8, the final sentence in the paragraph.
The lack of couplings in sentences 4, 6, and 7 is
more than made up for by the four that are compressed into sentence 2. As Brewster sweetly
departs this life unto a better--as he moves toward
God, so do the couplings.

Shaped and held tightly together by many
intrasentence connectives, this paragraph is
one of the clearest statements of Bradford's
argument: God is man's only alternative. The word
Lord simply dominates the paragraph; it occurs in
the beginning, middle, and end, allowing little
room for refutation of the argument. The paragraph
progresses from "the Lord Jesus and the gospel's
sake" in sentence 2 to "the Lord upheld him" and
"Lord" in sentences 3 and 4, and concludes with
"sweetly departed this life unto a better." The
references to England, Holland, and the American
wilderness capsulize the whole epic voyage. They
also remind one of the search for various alternatives to the "gross darkness of popery," Satan's
oppositions, deceitful Dutch seamen, "a fearful
storm at sea," "these savage barbarians," John
Lyford, and Thomas Morton. And Brewster's life
testifies vividly that there is only one.

As the contrasting incidents in chapter 9
concerning a "very profane young man" and John
Howland suggest, God rewards those who accept Him
as their only alternative. Ironically, the profane
young man falls victim to the very same thing that
he wishes upon the sick people aboard ship; he
becomes sick, dies, and is thrown overboard. Yet
Howland, one who acknowledges God as his only
alternative, ends up overboard too. But instead of
falling toward death, he falls toward rebirth:
"he lived many years after and became a profit-
able member both in church and commonwealth"
(p. 59). Like Howland's, Brewster's reward is a
long life: "the Lord upheld him to a great age."
In fact, the emphasis in the Brewster paragraph is
on life, not on death. Brewster doesn't die; he is
reborn. Everywhere the word die appears, it is

placed in a position that de-emphasizes it. Note, for instance, the first reference to "die" in sentence 2:

> About the 18th of April died their Reverend Elder and my dear and loving friend Mr. William Brewster, a man that had done and suffered much for the Lord Jesus and the gospel's sake, and had borne his part in weal and woe with this poor persecuted church above 36 years in England, Holland and in this wilderness, and done the Lord and them faithful service in his place and calling.

The fact that this is a periodic structure which inverts the usual order of the constituents in the English sentence (noun phrase, auxiliary, and verb phrase) causes the emphasis to fall on the noun phrase (their Reverend Elder and my dear and loving friend Mr. William Brewster) and the three parallel and balanced embedded sentences which follow it. The second reference to "die" takes place within a subordinate clause in sentence 4: "when he died." In sentence 5, Bradford places "die" in an infinitive phrase: "to die in bed." He no longer uses "die" in the last sentence, but employs instead simile and euphemism. Brewster is like a man who takes a long breath and falls into a sound sleep. He does not die; he sweetly departs this life unto a better.

"Daniel could be better liking with pulse than others were with the king's dainties. Jacob, though he went from one nation to another people and passed through famine, fears and many afflictions, yet he lived till old age and died sweetly and rested in the Lord," says Bradford a few paragraphs later. Brewster's life is analogous to Daniel's and Jacob's; their lives prefigure Brewster's. As the Lord rewarded them in their afflictions, He now rewards Brewster.

Brewster's life is also seen in terms of Christ's. The number of years (36) that Brewster works and suffers for "the Lord Jesus and the gospel's sake" is remarkably similar to the number of years Christ does essentially the same thing. Brewster's death recalls the crucifixion and the resurrection. The people "mourned and wept" his imminent death. Even when he knows that death is near, he continues to "recomfort them." Bradford takes great pains near the end of the paragraph to suggest that Brewster's death is no common or ordinary one. The detailed descriptions of the time of day, the absence of pain, and the manner of breathing lead directly to the word "sweet." At this point, Brewster and Christ become one. Both are on the Cross; both have suffered and died for the sins of their people. Their departure is sweet because they are moving toward a beautiful and enduring reward--a different and much better predicament. "I would now demand of any," says Bradford confidently, "what he was worse for any former sufferings?"

There is little genuine invisibility in this paragraph. If anything, it is invisibility re-called. The paragraph begins with the visible and factual. Brewster dies on April 18, 1643, after many years of striving and suffering for his people, his church, and his God. The references to England, Holland, and the wilderness recall the invisibility imposed by the "gross darkness of popery," Satan, storms, and the like, but this is all in the past. Brewster's life is like the "light of the gospel." Thus, the paragraph returns quickly to the present and visibility: "the Lord upheld him." There is little that is difficult to perceive about the manner and meaning of Brewster's death, as the details throughout the remainder of the paragraph make clear: his sickness is brief; he is not completely confined to bed; his speech fails him "about nine or ten a clock that evening"; he draws his "breath short" for a few hours; he draws "his breath long as a man fallen into a sound sleep" a few minutes before his last breath; and he dies painlessly.

When Brewster sweetly departs this life unto a better, surely his destination is God. The voyage

131

that he takes is representative of the voyage of
this entire history. There are many nouns and noun
phrases that are collocates of the nodal item
voyage. There are words which indicate the voyagers: "I," "Brewster," and "they"; words that are
related to time: "year," "April," "last day,"
"nine or ten a clock," "evening," "hours," and
minutes"; words which suggest various essentials to
have or carry on a journey: "Reverend Elder,"
"Lord," "faithful service," "rest," "bed," and
"peace"; words which suggest the purpose of the
voyage: "the Lord Jesus and the gospel's sake" and
"this poor persecuted church"; and words which
indicate the destination: "Holland," "this wilderness," "Lord," and "life." The progression of the
words related to destination provides a brief but
explicit synopsis of the Pilgrims' whole epic
journey. Sea of troubles includes such words as
"woe," "poor persecuted church," "England,"
"Holland," "wilderness," and "troubles and sorrows." Voyage and sea of troubles share some of
their collocates with Lord, but some significant
Lord words are "great age," "blessing," "rest,"
"peace," "help and comfort," and "life."

The nodal item verbs of sustaining dominates
the verbs and verbals: "upheld," which is the most
significant verb because it carries the main
concern of the paragraph, "done," "ministered," and
"recomforted." Of some importance too are the
travel related verbs and verbals: "to begin,"
"passed," "to die," "continued," and "departed."

Though not used extensively, alliterative
patterns provide unity and coherence. There is
the /m/ sound pattern in sentence 1 ("matter"
and "mourning"); in sentence 2 ("my," "main,"
and "much); in sentence 5 ("midst," "mourned,"
and "ministered"); and in sentence 8 ("minutes"
and "man"). There is the /d/ sound pattern in
sentences 2 ("died," "dear," and "done") and 8
("drew," "drew," and "departed"). There is the /w/
sound in sentence 2: "William," "weal and woe,"
and "wilderness"; the /s/ sound in sentence 8:
"some," "sound sleep," and "so sweetly"; and the

/p/ sound in sentence 2: "poor persecuted" and "place." Other words throughout the paragraph have the same initial sounds.

Things are not seen in antithetic relations in this paragraph; this biography or eulogy presents the life of a man who never loses sight of a single but sustaining belief or vision. This time (and as has been seen before), the paragraph gains balance and parallelism by the repetition of similar syntactic patterns. Most of the sentences adhere to the usual constituent order of the English sentence: sentences 1, 4, 5, 6, and 7. Others differ from the usual constituent order by beginning with some kind of introductory material, usually a prepositional phrase: sentences 2, 3, 5, and 8. In fact the latter part of sentence 2 contains a string of prepositional phrases: "in weal and woe with this poor persecuted church above 36 years in England, Holland and in this wilderness, and done the Lord and them faithful service in his place and calling." Long relative clauses are used twice: sentences 2 and 5. The paragraph ends with an almost perfectly balanced and parallel sentence: "A few hours before, he drew his breath short, and some few before his last, he drew his breath long as a man fallen into a sound sleep without any pangs or gaspings, and so sweetly departed this life unto a better." There are two parallel and balanced adverbial phrases and two parallel and balanced independent clauses. This sentence demonstrates a common device of parallelism and balance: the stringing together of similar syntactic patterns with a coordinating conjunction.

The repetition of words and phrases and the use of synonyms provide unity and coherence. "Mourn" is repeated twice and has many synonyms: "suffer" and "woe." "Sadness" has synonyms or collocates in "mourning," "suffered," "troubles and sorrows," and "mourned and wept." "Done" appears twice and has synonyms in "ministered" and "recomforted." "Lord" and "die" occur four times each.

"Pangs," "drew," and "breath" appear two times each.

The final two paragraphs come near the latter portion of chapter 33. Though Brewster is mentioned, Bradford is primarily interested in the long lives of all Pilgrim fathers. It is fitting that this chapter should conclude with these paragraphs for a number of reasons. There are, for instance, some interesting similarities between the foregrounded paragraphs and those that follow. The first line of the first foregrounded paragraph reads: "But here I cannot but stay and make a pause, and stand half amazed at this poor people's present condition; and so I think will the reader, too, when he well considers the same." Compare this with the first line of the first paragraph below: "I cannot but here take occasion not only to mention but greatly to admire the marvelous providence of God." The first four words of both sentences have the same phonological shape. In a reflective state mixed with amazement and admiration, the narrator "makes a pause" or "takes occasion" in both lines. In the first sentence, he ponders the plight of the Pilgrims after their sufferings in England, Holland, and the voyage to America. In the second sentence, he contemplates their sufferings after the whole American experience. The first sentence of the second foregrounded paragraph is: "What could now sustain them but the Spirit of God and His grace?" The first sentence of the second paragraph below is: "What was it then that upheld them?" While both are transitional sentences, they function more as rhetorical questions than anything else. Both are semantically similar.

These last two paragraphs represent the clearest and final statement of Bradford's argument. Adding to the details of the previous Brewster paragraph, they provide a thorough summary of the history. As such, they have many of the characteristics of a concluding chapter, although there are three additional chapters in the history. These paragraphs are:

I cannot but here take occasion not
only to mention but greatly to admire the
marvelous providence of God.   That notwithstanding the many changes and hardships that
these people went through, and the many
enemies they had and difficulties they met
withal, that so many of them should live to
very old age!   It was not only this reverend
man's condition (for one swallow makes no
summer as they say) but many more of them did
the like, some dying about and before this
time and many still living, who attained to
sixty years of age, and to sixty-five, divers
to seventy and above, and some near eighty as
he did.   It must needs be more than ordinary
and above natural reason, that so it should
be.   For it is found in experience that change
of air, famine or unwholesome food, much
drinking of water, sorrows and troubles, etc.,
all of them are enemies to health, causes of
many diseases, consumers of natural vigour and
the bodies of men, and shorteners of life.
And yet of all these things they had a large
part and suffered deeply in the same.   They
went from England to Holland, where they found
both worse air and diet than that they came
from; from thence, enduring a long imprisonment as it were in the ships at sea, into New
England; and how it hath been with them here
hath already been shown, and what crosses,
troubles, fears, wants and sorrows they had
been liable unto is easy to conjecture.   So as
in some sort they may say with the Apostle,
2 Corinthians x1.26.27, they were "in journeyings often, in perils of waters, in perils of
robbers, in perils of their own nation, in
perils among the heathen, in perils in the
wilderness, in perils in the sea, in perils
among false brethren; in weariness and painfulness, in watching often, in hunger and
thirst, in fasting often, in cold and nakedness."

What was it then that upheld them?   It
was God's visitation that preserved their

135

spirits. Job x.12: "Thou has given me life
and grace, and thy visitation hath preserved
my spirit." He that upheld the Apostle upheld
them. "They were persecuted, but not forsaken, cast down, but perished not." "As
unknown, yet known; as dying, and behold we
live; as chastened, and yet not killed";
2 Corinthians vi.9. (pp. 328-329)

By gradation, the stress groups in sentence 1,
paragraph 1, rise from an initial binary stress
group and end in a three-stress one:

I cannot but here / take occasion not only to
mention / but greatly to admire / the marvelous providence of God!

The stress groups of sentence 2 are 4, 2, 3, 3,
and 5:

That notwithstanding the many changes and
hardships / that these people went through, /
and the many enemies they had / and difficulties they met withal, / that so many of
them should live to very old age!

Sentence 3 divides into stress groups of 5, 4, 4,
4, 2, 4, 2, 3, and 2:

It was not only this reverend man's condition
/ (for one swallow makes no summer as they
say) / but many more of them did the like, /
some dying about and before this time / and
many still living, / who attained to sixty

136

years of age, / and to sixty-five, / divers to seventy and above, / and some near eighty as he did.

6 and 2 are the stress groups for sentence 4, as Bradford compresses his amazement into a very short sentence, marking a significant moment in the paragraph:

It must needs be more than ordinary and above natural reason, / that so it should be.

The stress groups of sentence 5 are 2, 2, 3, 2, 2, 3, 2, 3, 2, and 2:

For it is found in experience / that change of air, / famine or unwholesome food, / much drinking of water, / sorrows and troubles, etc., / all of them are enemies to health, / causes of many diseases, / consumers of natural vigour / and the bodies of men, / and shorteners of life.

The stress groups of sentence 6 (2, 2, and 3) rise, matching the image of expansion:

And yet of all these things / they had a large part / and suffered deeply in the same.

The stress groups of sentence 7 are 3, 4, 2, 1, 3, 1, 2, 2, 3, 2, 1, 1, 1, 2, 3, and 2:

They went from England to Holland, / where they found both worse air and diet / than that

137

they came from; / from thence, / enduring a
long imprisonment / as it were , / in the ships
at sea, / into New England; / and how it hath
been with them here , / hath already been shown,
/ and what crosses, / troubles, / fears, /
wants and sorrows , / they had been liable unto
/ is easy to conjecture.

Containing a quotation from the Bible, sentence 8 rises and falls toward the second paragraph
or toward God: 5, 3, 2, 2, 2, 3, 2, 2, 3, 2, 2, 2,
2, and 2:

So as in some sort they may say with the
Apostle, 2 Corinthians x1.26,27, / they were
"in journeyings often, / in perils of waters,
/ in perils of robbers, / in perils of their
own nation, / in perils among the heathen, /
in perils in the wilderness, / in perils in
the sea, / in perils among false brethren; /
in weariness and painfulness, / in watching
often, / in hunger and thirst, / in fasting
often, / in cold and nakedness."

The manner in which this quotation divides easily
into binay stress groups serves as a vivid reminder
that the Bible is a major source of Bradford's
style, especially his rhythm.

Paragraph 1 contains many couplings and
coordinate pairs that create similar effects as the

couplings: "to mention but greatly to admire," "changes and hardships," "about and before," "more than ordinary and above natural reason," "sorrows and troubles," "had a large part and suffered," "air and diet," "wants and sorrows," "weariness and painfulness," "hunger and thirst," and "cold and nakedness." Paragraph 2 contains the coupling-like "life and grace."

These paragraphs represent one of the most moving and beautiful moments in the history, an impression generated by the interplay of the two-part series (the couplings and other coordinate pairs) and the four-or-more part series. In the first paragraph, the two-part series takes control: "change of air, famine or unwholesome food, much drinking of water, sorrows and troubles, etc., all of them are enemies to health, causes of many diseases, consumers of natural vigour and the bodies of men, and shorteners of life," suggesting the human, emotional, diffuse, and inexplicable. In sentence 6 and the early part of 7, the two-part series regains control, only to lose it to the beautiful catalog of events in the latter parts of sentences 7 and 8: "what crosses, troubles, fears, wants and sorrows; and "'in journeyings often, in perils of waters, in perils of robbers, in perils of their own nation,'" etc. The completion of the almost impossible and incredible journey is something to "stand half amazed at," and the four-or-more part series does much in creating the aura of amazement.

Few places in the history demonstrate the relationship between the connectives and Bradford's argument better than paragraph 1. Although there are many connectives in the paragraph, three shape and control the argument: "for" at the beginning of sentence 5, "and yet" at the beginning of sentence 6, and "so" at the beginning of 8. The connectives cause these three sentences to function much like a categorical syllogism. Sentence 5 is the major premise: using experience as a basis, it cites all things that shorten life. Sentence 6 is the minor premise: it suggests that the Pilgrims

139

have experienced all things that shorten life. Sentence 8 is the conclusion: "so" takes on the effect of "therefore" as Bradford seeks biblical explanation for the paradox which emerges from sentences 5 and 6. Sentence 2, paragraph 2, provides the explanation in no unclear terms: "It was God's visitation that preserved their spirits."

Many biblical parallels run throughout paragraph 1. All rush toward paragraph 2 or toward God. There is the standard analogy between the exodus from Egypt and the exodus from England and Holland in sentence 7. Like Brewster's, the lives of the other Pilgrim fathers re-enact those of Daniel and Jacob. The Pilgrims also re-enact Paul, as sentence 8, paragraph 1, and the majority of paragraph 2 indicate. And finally, the many references to the Pilgrims' sufferings and hardships, particularly the reference to "crosses" in sentence 7, paragraph 1, recall Christ's sufferings.

As in the Brewster paragraph, invisibility exists, but only in the sense that the paragraphs look back to previous states of invisibility. For instance, sentence 1, paragraph 1 speaks of that which is clearly visible, the "marvelous providence of God." Beginning with the reference to "changes and hardships" in sentence 2 however, the emphasis is shifted back to the past, back to the previous states of complexity and invisibility: this was a period of "many enemies" and "difficulties"; the Pilgrims experienced many things that shortened life; they experienced worse air and diet in Holland than in England; they endured a lengthy imprisonment in their ship at sea; they met a hostile nature and savage natives upon landing at Cape Cod, not to mention the many difficulties that surfaced as they sought to tame the American wilderness and establish communities. But sentence 8 and paragraph 2 return to the present and bring with them the visibility that comes from the knowledge and certainty that God is man's only lasting alternative, that He upholds and preserves all of his servants. He is a timeless, life-giving force.

140

As He upheld Moses, Daniel, and Jacob, He upholds the Pilgrim fathers. And as He upholds the Pilgrim fathers, he will uphold the "children of these fathers," if they take the stance, as Bradford surely does, that one should trust and rely solely on God.

Most words can be grouped around the nodal items voyage, sea of troubles, and Lord fairly easily. Although there are nouns and noun phrases which suggest a voyage (e.g., England, Holland, long imprisonment in ships at sea, and journeyings), the idea of a journey is carried mainly by the verbs: "went through," "attained," "is found," "went," "found," and "came from." Sea of troubles includes all words that are negative in tone, and there are many of them: "enemies," "famine," "unwholesome food," "sorrows and troubles," "diseases," "crosses," "fears," etc. Lord includes all positive words, particularly those words in paragraph 2: "upheld," "God's visitation," "preserved," "life," etc. While collocation is helpful, what proves most beneficial is a simple list of all nouns and verbs. From this list, a clear sense of the relationship between paragraphs 1 and 2--a clear sense of paragraph movement becomes visible. The nouns and verbs of paragraph 1 contrast sharply with those of paragraph 2. The many nouns with negative connotations in paragraph 1 (enemies, difficulties, diseases, imprisonments, wants and sorrows, perils, robbers, etc.) are offset by the many positive ones in paragraph 2 (God's visitation, their spirits, life, grace, God, and Apostle). The verb suffer in paragraph 1 sums up much of the Pilgrim experience, yet it too is offset by the many positive verbs in paragraph 2: "upheld," "preserved," "hast given," "not forsaken," "perished not," "live," and "not killed." This negative-positive movement is also another characteristic which these paragraphs and the foregrounded paragraphs have in common.

Most of the alliterative patterns occur in paragraph 1. There is the alliterative /m/ sound in sentence 1: "mention" and "marvelous"; in

sentence 2: "many," "many," "met," and "many"; and
in sentence 3: "man's," "makes," "many more," and
"many." There is the /s/ sound pattern in sentence 3: "swallow," "summer," "say," "some,"
"sixty," "sixty-five," "seventy," and "some"; in
sentence 6: "suffered" and "same"; and in sentence 8: "so," "some," "sort," "say," and "sea."
There is the /g/ sound in sentence 1: "greatly"
and "God" and the /f/ sound in sentence 5: "for,"
"found," "famine," and "food"; and in sentence 8:
"false" and "fasting." There is the /w/ sound
pattern in sentence 7: "went," "worse," "were,"
and "with"; and in sentence 8: "were," "waters,"
"wilderness," "weariness," and "watching."

There are some examples of assonance, but it
does not seem to play a major role: "providence"
and "God" in sentence 1; "makes" and "say" and
"still" and "living" in sentence 3; "needs," "be,"
and "reason" in sentence 4; and "large" and "part"
in sentence 6.

The "not only but also" correlatives in
sentences 1 and 2, paragraph 1, contribute to
balance and parallelism: "not only to mention but
greatly to admire"; and "not only this reverend
man's condition (for one swallow makes no summer as
they say) but many more of them did the like." In
both cases, "also" is understood. The repetition
of prepositional phrases is one of Bradford's
favorite devices of unity and coherence and the
anaphoric repetition of the "in perils" phrase at
the end of sentence 8 provides an excellent example
of this. Few places in the history contain better
examples of antithesis than sentences 5 and 6,
paragraph 2: "'They were persecuted, but not
forsaken, cast down, but perished not.' 'As
unknown, yet known; as dying, and behold we live;
as chastened, and yet not killed.'" These sentences provide a succinct and precise summation of
the paradoxical situations the Pilgrims found
themselves in.

Repetition is used extensively. "Many"
appears six times. "Changes," "enemies," "age,"

"sorrows," "waters," and "troubles" all occur
twice. In addition, "troubles" has numerous
synonyms and collocates: "hardships," "difficulties," "famine," "diseases," "crosses,"
"suffered," "robbers," "sea," "false brethren,"
"hunger," "thirst," "cold," "nakedness," and
"perils." The unified and coherent structure of
these paragraphs, and all paragraphs in the history, is simply remarkable.

It should be clear at this point how closely
aspects of style are related to aspects of structure and meaning. The many intrasentence details
of the foregrounded paragraphs grow into larger
intersentence ones, giving the foregrounded paragraphs several levels of meaning and structure.
The foregrounded passages, in turn, provide patterns of structure and meaning for other paragraphs, thus culminating in the structure of the
whole of Of Plymouth Plantation.

Notes to Chapter 4

[1] "'With my owne eyes': William Bradford's _Of Plymouth Plantation_, p. 99.

[2] "William Bradford Versus Thomas Morton," _Early American Literature_, 5, No. 2 (1970), 4-9.

[3] See D'Angelo's "Style as Structure," p. 351.

Conclusion

Although <u>Of Plymouth Plantation</u> comes to an
abrupt conclusion in 1647, this has little or no
effect on unity, coherence, meaning, and structure.
The book is tightly constructed in a unique and
untraditional manner, which is most probably
conscious on the part of Bradford, as the many
couplings, alliterative patterns, and the almost
metrical regularity of many passages strongly
indicate. It contains a stylistic center the
stylistic features of which establish patterns of
coherence, unity, meaning, and structure for all
preceding and succeeding paragraphs.

The one continuous, enduring structural
progression is the voyage toward God with all its
manifold aspects. Practically every paragraph in
the history concludes with a reference to God.
Perhaps the major concern of the book can best be
stated in question form: on this voyage toward
God, how does one cope with invisibility, with
complexity, with ambiguity--in short, with the sea
of troubles; how does one see, how does one find
alternatives to one's predicament? Seeing, un-
raveling complexity and ambiguity, finding alternatives, it seems to me, are among the chief concerns
of the history.

The pattern of visibility and invisibility is
set in the very first sentence of the history:

> It is well known unto the godly and judicious,
> how ever since the first breaking out of the
> light of the gospel in our honourable nation
> of England, (which was the first of nations
> whom the Lord adorned therewith after the
> gross darkness of popery which had covered and
> overspread the Christian world), what wars and
> oppositions ever since, Satan hath raised,
> maintained and continued against the Saints,
> from time to time in one sort or other.
> (p. 3)

These contrasting pairs (God vs. Satan, Saints vs. Satan, good vs. evil, and light vs. dark) give form and control to many other passages. The arrival, for example, of the Dutch seaman to take the Pilgrims to Holland is described in light-dark terms: "So after long waiting and large expenses, though he kept not day with them, yet he came at length and took them in, in the night" (p. 12). On one of the many scouting expeditions, Bradford sees the planters as people of the day and the Indians as sly, beast-like people of the night:

> So they [the scouting expedition] ranged up and down all that day, but found no people, nor any place they liked. When the sun grew low, they hasted out of the woods to meet with their shallop, to whom they made signs to come to them into a creek hard by, the which they did at high water; of which they were very glad, for they had not seen each other all that day since the morning. So they made them a barricado as usually they did every night, with logs, stakes and thick pine boughs, the height of a man, leaving it open to leeward, partly to shelter them from the cold and wind . . . and partly to defend them from any sudden assaults of the savages, if they should surround them; so being very weary, they betook them to rest. But about midnight they heard a hideous and great cry, and their sentinel called "Arm! arm!" So they bestirred them and stood to their arms and shot off a couple of muskets, and then the noise ceased. They concluded it was a company of wolves or such like wild beasts, for one of the seamen told them he had often heard such a noise in Newfoundland. (p. 69)

A few moments later, one discovers that these wild beasts of darkness are Indians, as the scouting party must surely have known from the start.

Summing up the progress of the Pilgrim settlement in one of the most famous passages in the history, Bradford unconsciously expresses a desire for light to expose and defeat darkness:

146

Thus out of small beginnings greater things have been produced by His hand that made all things of nothing, and gives being to all things that are; and as one candle may light a thousand, so the light here kindled hath shone unto many, yea in some sort to our whole nation; let the glorious name of Jehovah have all the praise. (p. 236)

A major source of complexity and ambiguity is Satan's ability to change his form and methods of assault:

For to let pass the infinite examples in sundry nations and several places of the world, and instance in our own, when as that old serpent could not prevail by those fiery flames and other his cruel tragedies, which he by his instruments put in ure everywhere in the days of Queen Mary and before, he then began another kind of war and went more closely to work; not only to oppugn but even to ruinate and destroy the kingdom of Christ by more secret and subtle means, by kindling the flames of contention and sowing the seeds of discord and bitter enimity amongst the professors and, seeming reformed, themselves. For when he could not prevail by the former means against the principal doctrines of faith, he bent his force against the holy discipline and outward regiment of the kingdom of Christ, by which those holy doctrines should be conserved, and true piety maintained amongst the saints and people of God. (p. 5)

Though the martial metaphor is not always this evident, each remaining major episode presents one of Satan's forms and methods; each presents a sea of troubles--something to find an alternative to--something that must be conquered before God can be reached. Satan takes the form of the many adventurers and their deceptive legal agreements with the Pilgrims. Chief among the adventurers is Thomas Weston, who alters the contract even before

147

the Pilgrims depart for Holland. After settling in
America, the planters are constantly confronted
with Weston's false charges of negligence. His
relief ships bring burdens instead of aid; they
deliver broken promises rather than the goods
necessary for survival. Weston finally sells out
to other adventurers who continue his exploitation.
But he does not end his deceptive practices. When
he comes to America, he does so under an alias and
the disguise of a blacksmith: "Shortly after,
Mr. Weston came over with some of the fishermen,
under another name, and the disguise of a blacksmith, where he heard of the ruin and dissolution
of his colony" (p. 119). Also, there is Allerton,
another adventurer whose avarice leads the planters
deeper into debt.

Satan appears in the form of the string of
poorly qualified ministers who plague the planters;
in the forms of starvation, sickness, and disease;
in the form of commercial success and prosperity
which cause a spiritual loss and the separation of
the community and the church; in the form of the
French who raid and capture the Pilgrims' trading
post; in the form of the first murder, the first
execution, and the first prison; in the form of
bestiality:

There was a youth whose name was Thomas
Granger. He was a servant to an honest man of
Duxbury, being about 16 or 17 years of age.
(His father and mother lived at the same time
at Scituate.) He was this year detected of
buggery, and indicted for the same, with a
mare, a cow, two goats, five sheep, two calves
and a turkey. (p. 320)

And of course, one should not forget Lyford,
Oldham, and Morton. Bradford's constant warning of
the vanity of placing one's trust in man and
material things shows his acute awareness of
Satan's subtlety. Bradford knows that man and
material things are two of Satan's favorite dis-
guises. Above all, he knows that it is practically
impossible to discern the real man, even in the

148

regenerate. "A man's way," says Bradford, "is not in his own power" (pp. 118-119). "The mutable things of this unstable world" are so uncertain (p. 119). "Man may purpose, but God doth dispose" (p. 180). The reader cannot help appreciating the complexity and ambiguity of Bradford's world, if not from such cogent statements like the preceding ones, then certainly from the difficulty of finding antecedents to many of his pronouns and nouns.

The key to style in the history is repetition. Almost without exception, those things which are repeated grow into patterns of meaning and structure. Two chapters before the end of the history, Bradford provides one final statement of his argument:

> And thus was this poor church left, like an ancient mother grown old and forsaken of her children, though not in their affections yet in regard of their bodily presence and personal helpfulness; her ancient members being most of them worn away by death, and these of later time being like children translated into other families, and she like a widow left only to trust in God. (p. 334)

At this point in time, the church, like the history, has no other alternative but God.

With a good deal of justification, many critics have made much of another structural pattern which results from a change in tone. They argue that the history progresses from a tone of certainty to one of uncertainty. Although many passages are used to support the argument, it usually centers on Bradford's very different reactions to two similar moments in the history. The first moment occurs early in the history and concerns the "profane young man" who curses the sick aboard ship, hoping that they will die. "But," remarks Bradford,

> it pleased God before they came half seas over, to smite this young man with a grievous

disease, of which he died in a desperate manner, and so was himself the first that was thrown overboard. Thus his curses light on his own head, and it was an astonishment to all his fellows for they noted it to be the just hand of God upon him. (p. 58)

The absolute certainty that God punished the profane young man is absent from the second moment, which appears in the final chapter of the history and concerns Captain Thomas Cromwell, who kills one of his subordinates with a sword:

And there died the same summer, having got a fall from his horse, in which fall he fell on his rapier and so bruised his body as he shortly after died thereof, with some other distempers which brought him into a fever. Some observed that there might be something of the hand of God herein; that as the forenamed man died of the blow he gave him with the rapier hilt, so his own death was occasioned by a like means. (p. 346)

While the change in tone from "they noted it to be the just hand of God upon him" to "some observed that there might be something of the hand of God herein" is irrefutable, it does not constitute a flaw; it is not inconsistent with the structural progression of the history. The whole issue of tone hinges upon the nature of that which Bradford is uncertain of. He is uncertain of the Pilgrims' role as the chosen people, and that is all. He never wavers in his conviction that God is man's only alternative. When all else fails him, man, like the poor deserted church, can only "trust in God." The fact that Bradford can no longer write confidently of the Pilgrims' role as a biblically sanctioned and special one humbles him. Thus, the uncertainty that one sees as the book progresses toward the final chapters is positive, not negative. Organizing, including, omitting, and interpreting historical events in the early parts of the history at will, Bradford shows too much certainty, too much pride in the Pilgrims as a special people. At times, he seems to boast with a slight air of arrogance. But the many troubles make Bradford aware of his own humanness, his own vulnerability:

> Which will be made manifest, if the Lord be pleased to give life and time. In the meantime I cannot but admire His ways and works towards His servants, and humbly desire to bless His holy name for His great mercies hitherto (p. 215)

and "As will appear if God give life to finish this history" (p. 236). The troubles purge him of his pride and leave him in a state of humility. It is in this state that Bradford and the rest of the Pilgrims are closest to God because they are most receptive to Him. Therefore, one can say that the tone moves toward God because it progresses from certainty to an uncertainty that is tied tightly to humility.

In the final analysis, Bradford's style is quite deceptive; it has all of the appearances of simplicity when it is actually very complex. For example, a close examination of the stylistic devices in the preface will reveal that even its style is not "plain" and "simple" in any sense of the words: complex alliterative patterns, couplings (some of which are alliterative), assonance, extensive repetition of words and phrases, balance and parallelism--all of these in just two sentences. Many stylistic devices promote meaning and structure throughout the book. While I make no claim to having discovered them all, I do feel that I have discussed enough to prove that Of Plymouth Plantation is a rich and tightly organized work which deserves its current status among seminal American works.

Notes to Conclusion

[1] See footnote 1 in chapter 2.

Bibliography

Baum, Paull Franklin. . . . the other harmony of prose. . . . Durham, N. C.: Duke University Press, 1952.

Bennett, James R., ed. Prose Style: A Historical Approach through Studies. San Francisco: Chandler Publishing Co., 1971.

Bercovitch, Sacvan, ed. Typology and Early American Literature. Amherst: The University of Massachusetts Press, 1972.

----------. "Typology in Puritan New England: The Williams-Cotton Controversy Reassessed." American Quarterly, 19 (Summer, 1967), 166-191.

Boulton, Marjorie. The Anatomy of Prose. London: Routledge and Kegan Paul, 1954.

Bradford, E. F. "Conscious Art in Bradford's History of Plymouth Plantation." New England Quarterly, 1 (1928), 133-157.

Bradford, William. Of Plymouth Plantation 1620-1647. Ed. Samuel E. Morison. New York: The Modern Library, 1952.

Bridgman, Richard. The Colloquial Style in America. New York: Oxford University Press, 1966.

Brumm, Ursula. "Did the Pilgrims Fall upon Their Knees When They Arrived in the New World? Art and History in the Ninth Chapter, Book One, of Bradford's History Of Plymouth Plantation." Early American Literature, 12, No. 1 (1977), 25-35.

Cappel, William. "Repetition in the Language of Fiction." Style, 4, No. 3 (1970), 239-244.

Carpenter, Ronald H. "Stylistic Redundancy and Function in Discourse." Language and Style, 3, No. 1 (1970), 62-68.

Carson, Julie. "Proper Stylistics." Style, 8 (Spring, 1974), 290-305.

Cass, Colin S. "Two Stylistic Analyses of the Narrative Prose in Cozzens' By Love Possessed." Style, 4, No. 3 (1970), 213-238.

Chatman, Seymour. "New Ways of Analyzing Narrative Structure." Language and Style, 2 (1969), 1-36.

----------. "Stylistics Quantitative and Qualitative." Style, 1, No. 1 (1967), 29-43.

Christensen, Francis. Notes Toward a New Rhetoric: Six Essays for Teachers. New York: Harper and Row, 1967.

Classe, André. The Rhythm of English Prose. Oxford: Basil Blackwell, 1939.

Corbett, Edward P. J. Classic Rhetoric for the Modern Student. New York: Oxford University Press, 1971.

----------. "A Method of Analyzing Prose Style with a Demonstration Analysis of Swift's 'A Modest Proposal.'" In Contemporary Essays on Style. Eds. Glen A. Love and Michael Payne. Glenview, Ill.: Scott, Foresman and Co., 1969, pp. 81-98.

Cummings, D. W., John Herum, and E. K. Lybbert. "Semantic Recurrence and Rhetorical Form." Language and Style, 4, No. 3 (1971), 195-207.

Cunningham, Donald. "Analyzing Paragraph Structure." Exercise Exchange, 16 (1971), 8-9.

Daley, Robert. "William Bradford's Vision of History." American Literature, 44 (Jan., 1973), 557-569.

D'Angelo, Frank. "A Generative Rhetoric of the Essay." College Composition and Communication, 25 (Dec. 1974), 388-396.

----------. "Imitation and Style." College Composition and Communication, 24 (Oct. 1973), 283-290.

----------. "Style as Structure." Style, 8, No. 2 (1974), 322-362.

Delisle, Harold. "Style and Idea in Steinbeck's 'The Turtle.'" Style, 4 (1970), 145-154.

Elliott, Emory. "From Father to Son: the Evolution of Typology in Puritan New England." In Literary Uses of Typology. Ed. Earl Minor. Princeton: Princeton University Press, 1977, pp. 201-227.

Enkvist, Nils Erik. "On the Place of Style in Some Linguistic Theories." In Literary Style: A Symposium. Ed. S. Chatman. New York: Oxford University Press, 1971, pp. 47-65.

Firth, J. R. Papers in Linguistics 1934-1951. London: Oxford University Press, 1957, pp. 190-214.

Fritscher, John J. "The Sensibility and Conscious Style of William Bradford." Bucknell Review, 17 (1969), 80-90.

Froehlich, Karlfried. "'Always to Keep the Literal Sense in Holy Scripture Means to Kill One's Soul': the State of Biblical Hermeneutics at the Beginning of the Fifteenth Century." In Literary Uses of Typology. Ed. Earl Minor. Princeton: Princeton University Press, 1977, pp. 20-48.

Gallagher, Edward and Thomas Werge. Early Puritan
    Writers: William Bradford, John Cotton,
    Thomas Hooker, Edward Johnson, Richard Mather,
    and Thomas Shepard. Boston: G. K. Hall,
    1976.

Gay, Peter. A Loss of Mastery: Puritan Historians
    in Colonial America. Berkeley: University of
    California Press, 1966.

Gordon, Ian.   The Movement of English Prose.
    London: Longmans, 1966.

Grady, Michael. "On Teaching Christensen Rhetoric"
    English Journal, 61 (1972), 859-877.

Griffith, John.   "Of Plymouth Plantation as a
    Mercantile Epic." Arizona Quarterly, 28
    (Autumn, 1972), 231-242.

Heller, L. G. "The Structural Relationship between
    Theme and Characterization." Language and
    Style, 4 No. 2 (1971), 123-130.

Hollander, Robert. "Typology and Secular Litera-
    ture: Some Medieval Problems and Examples."
    In Literary Uses of Typology. Ed. Earl Minor.
    Princeton: Princeton University Press,
    1977, pp. 3-19.

Hoover, Regina M. "Prose Rhythm: A Theory of
    Proportional Distribution." College Composi-
    tion and Communication, 24 (Dec. 1973),
    366-374.

Hovey, Kenneth Alan. "The Theology of History in
    Of Plymouth Plantaton and Its Predecessors."
    Early American Literature, 10, No. 1 (1975),
    47-66.

Howard, Alan B. "Art and History in Bradford's Of
    Plymouth Plantation." William and Mary
    Quarterly, 28 (1971), 237-266.

Jones, Howard Mumford. _Ideas in America_. Cambridge: Harvard University Press, 1945.

----------. _O Strange New World_. New York: The Viking Press, 1952.

Kligerman, Jack. "A Stylistic Approach to Hawthorne's 'Roger Malvin's Burial.'" _Language and Style_, 4, No. 3 (1971), 188-194.

Korshin, Paul J. "The Development of Abstracted Typology in England, 1650-1820." In _Literary Uses of Typology_. Ed. Earl Minor. Princeton: Princeton University Press, 1977, pp. 147-203.

Kraus, Michael. _The Writing of American History_. Norman, Okla.: University of Oklahoma Press, 1953.

Leech, G. N. "Linguistics and the Figures of Rhetoric." In _Essays on Style and Language_. Ed. Roger Fowler. London: Routledge and Kegan Paul, 1966.

----------. "'This bread I break'--Language and Interpretation." _A Review of English Literature_, 6, No. 2 (1965), 66-75.

Levin, David. "William Bradford: The Value of Puritan Historiography." In _Major Writers of Early American Literature_. Ed. Everett A. Emerson. Madison: University of Wisconsin Press, 1972, pp. 11-31.

Lowance, Mason I., Jr. "Typology and Millennial Eschatology in Early New England." In _Literary Uses of Typology_. Ed. Earl Minor. Princeton: Princeton University Press, 1977, pp. 228-273.

Lynen, John F. _The Design of the Present: Essays on Time and Form in American Literature_. New Haven: Yale University Press, 1969.

Major, Minor W. "William Bradford Versus Thomas
    Morton." Early American Literature, 5, No. 2
    (1970), 1-13.

Marckwardt, Albert H. American English. New York:
    Oxford University Press, 1958.

Martin, Harold C. "The Development of Style in
    Ninteenth-Century American Fiction." In Style
    in Prose Fiction: English Institute Essays
    1958. New York, 1959, pp. 114-141.

McConnell, Frank D. "Toward a Syntax of Fiction."
    College English, 36 (Oct. 1974), 147-160.

McLain, Richard. "The Problem of 'Style': Another
    Case in Fuzzy Grammar." Language and Style,
    10, No. 1 (1977), 52-65.

Miles, Josephine. Style and Proportion: The
    Language of Prose and Poetry. Boston: Little
    Brown and Co., 1967.

Milic, Louis T. "Connectives in Swift's Prose
    Style." In Linguistics and Literary Style.
    Ed. Donald C. Freeman. New York: Holt,
    Rhinehart and Winston, 1970, pp. 243-255.

Murdock, Kenneth B. "Colonial Historians." In
    American Writers on American Literature. Ed.
    John Macy. New York: Tudor Publishing Co.,
    1931, pp. 3-12.

----------. "The Colonial and Revolutionary
    Period." In The Literature of the American
    People. Ed. Arthur H. Quinn. New York:
    Appleton-Century Crofts, 1929.

Ohmann, Richard. "Generative Grammars and the
    Concept of Literary Style." In Linguistics
    and Literary Style. Ed. Donald C. Freeman.
    New York: Holt, Rhinehart and Winston, 1970,
    pp. 258-278.

----------. "Literature as Sentences." In <u>Essays on the Language of Literature</u>. Ed. S. Chatman and S. R. Levin. Boston: Houghton Mifflin Co., 1967, pp. 231-238.

----------. "Speech, Action, and Style." In <u>Literary Symposium</u>. New York: Oxford University Press, 1971, pp. 241-254.

Orth, Michael. "The Prose Style of Henry David Thoreau." <u>Language and Style</u>, 7 (1974), 36-52.

Poirier, Richard. <u>A World Elsewhere: the Place of Style in American Literature</u>. New York: Oxford University Press, 1966.

Ross, Donald J. "Composition as a Stylistic Feature." <u>Style</u>, 4 (1970), 1-10.

Ross, Robert N. "Conceptual Network Analysis." <u>Semiotica</u>, 10 (1974), 1-17.

Saintsbury, George. <u>A History of English Prose Rhythm</u>. 3rd ed., 1912; rpt. Bloomington: Indiana University Press, 1967.

Sayce, N. A. "Literature and Language." <u>Essays in Criticism</u>, 7 (April 1957), 119-133.

Scheick, William. "The Theme of Necessity in Bradford's <u>Of Plymouth Plantation</u>." <u>Seventeenth Century News</u>, 32, No. 4 (1974), 88-90.

Scholes, Robert. <u>Structuralism in Literature</u>. New Haven: Yale University Press, 1974.

Shea, Daniel. <u>Spiritual Autobiography in Early American Literature</u>. Princeton: Princeton University Press, 1968.

Short, M. H. "Some Thoughts on Foregrounding and Interpretation." <u>Language and Style</u>, 6 (1973), 97-108.

Smith, Bradford. _Bradford of Plymouth_. Phila-
     delphia: Lippincott, 1951.

Spencer, John and Michael Gregory. "An Approach to
     the Study of Style." In _Lingusitics and
     Style_. Ed. John Spencer. London: Oxford
     University Press, 1964, pp. 59-105.

Walker, Robert L. "The Common Writer: A Case for
     Parallel Structure." _College Composition and
     Communication_, 21 (Dec. 1970), 373-379.

Watt, Ian. "The First Paragraph of _The Ambas-
     sadors_: An Explication." In _Essays in
     Stylistic Analysis_. Ed. Howard S. Babb. New
     York: Harcourt Brace Jovanovich, 1972,
     pp. 275-292.

Weathers, Winston. "The Rhetoric of the Series."
     In _Contemporary Essays on Style_. Ed. Glen A.
     Love and Michael Payne. Glenview, Ill.:
     Scott Foresman and Co., 1969, pp. 21-27.

Wells, Rulon. "Nominal and Verbal Style." In _The
     Problem of Style_. Ed. J. V. Cunningham.
     Greenwich: Fawcett, 1966, pp. 253-259.

Woodman, Leonora. "A Lingustic Approach to Prose
     Style." _English Journal_, 62 (April 1973),
     587-603.

INDEX

161

Index continued

Index continued

Unity and Coherence